CAMBRIDGE TEXTBOOKS IN LINGUISTICS

General Editors: W.SIDNEY ALLEN, C.J.FILLMORE
EUGENIE J.A.HENDERSON, FRED W.HOUSEHOLDER, JOHN LYONS
R.B.LE PAGE, F.R.PALMER, J.L.M.TRIM

LOGIC IN LINGUISTICS

Already published in the series:
Morphology, by P. H. Matthews
Aspect, by Bernard Comrie
Semantics, by R. Kempson
Historical Linguistics, by T. Bynon
Other titles are in preparation.

LOGIC IN LINGUISTICS

JENS ALLWOOD
LARS-GUNNAR ANDERSSON
ÖSTEN DAHL

CAMBRIDGE UNIVERSITY PRESS
CAMBRIDGE
LONDON · NEW YORK · MELBOURNE

Published by the Syndics of the Cambridge University Press
The Pitt Building, Trumpington Street, Cambridge CB2 1RP
Bentley House, 200 Euston Road, London NW1 2DB
32 East 57th Street, New York, NY 10022, USA
296 Beaconsfield Parade, Middle Park, Melbourne 3206, Australia

First published in English translation 1977

Printed in Great Britain at the
University Press, Cambridge

ISBN 0 521 21496 3   hard covers
ISBN 0 521 29174 7   paperback

CONTENTS

Preface viii   *Symbols and notational conventions.* ix

1   Logic for linguists   *page* 1

2   Set theory   3
2.1   *Sets and elements*   3
2.2   *Relations between sets*   5
2.3   *Operations on sets*   6
2.4   *Relations and functions*   9

3   Inference and logical analysis of sentences   15
3.1   *Inference*   15
3.2   *Logical form*   18
3.3   *Sentences and propositions*   20
3.4   *Possible worlds and the truth-set of a proposition*   22
3.5   *Analytic and synthetic sentences*   23
3.6   *Simple and compound sentences*   24
3.7   *The depth of the logical analysis*   25

4   Propositional logic   26
4.1   *Connectives*   26
4.2   *The meaning of the logical connectives*   30
4.2.1   *Negation*   30
4.2.2   *Conjunction*   32
4.2.3   *Disjunction*   34
4.2.4   *Implication*   37
4.2.5   *Equivalence*   40
4.3   *How to indicate constituent structure*   42
4.4   *The syntax and semantics of propositional calculus*   44
4.5   *Syntax*   45
4.6   *Semantics*   47
4.7   *Tautologies and contradictions*   50
4.8   *Truth tables*   50

5	Predicate logic	*page* 58
5.1	*Extending the logical analysis*	58
5.2	*Quantifiers*	61
5.3	*Summary of the syntax of predicate logic*	71
5.4	*The semantics of predicate logic*	72
5.5	*True in all interpretations*	77
5.6	*Summary of the semantics of predicate logic*	83
5.7	*A formal version of the semantics*	84
5.8	*Formal properties of relations*	88
5.8.1	*Reflexivity*	88
5.8.2	*Symmetry*	89
5.8.3	*Transitivity*	89
5.8.4	*Converse*	90
5.8.5	*Structure of the domain and co-domain of relations*	90

6	Deduction	96
6.1	*The deductive system*	96
6.2	*Deduction rules in everyday conversation*	104

7	Modal logic	108
7.1	*Modal operators*	108
7.2	*Strict implication*	110
7.3	*Other modalities*	111
7.4	*Problems connected with scope and identity in modal logic*	114
7.4.1	*'De dicto'–'de re' ambiguities*	114
7.4.2	*Specificity*	116
7.4.3	*Opacity*	117
7.4.4.	*Cross-world identification*	119
7.5	*Counterfactual sentences*	120
7.6	*Tense logic and reference points*	121

8	Intensional logic and categorial grammar	125
8.1	*Intensions and extensions*	125
8.2	*Intension*	127
8.3	*The Fregean principle*	130
8.4	*The Fregean principle and categorial grammar*	132
8.5	*Categories, intensions and types*	136

9	Further extensions	148
9.1	*Second-order predicate logic and predicate operators*	148
9.2	*Presuppositions and definite descriptions*	149
9.3	*Pragmatic analysis of presuppositions*	153
9.4	*The abstraction- or lambda-operator*	155

10	Logic for linguists?	page	158
10.1	*General*		158
10.2	*The concept of meaning*		158
10.3	*The role of formal languages in analysing natural language*		164
10.4	*The limitations of classical logic*		168
	References		172
	Answers to exercises		175
	Index		181

PREFACE

This book has grown out of an introduction to logic for linguists in Swedish published by Studentlitteratur, Lund, 1971, a German translation of which appeared in 1973 (Niemeyer Verlag). All the chapters of the Swedish book have been revised and several additions (including the whole of chapter 8) have been made. The goal is still the same: to give linguists and others interested in language an orientation in logic which will enable them to understand how logical concepts are used (or could be used) in linguistic theory, in particular semantics.

We have benefited from suggestions and critical remarks made by several people. In addition to several generations of students at the Department of Linguistics in Göteborg, who have had to act as our guinea-pigs, we want to thank Claes Åberg, who has read the book in manuscript at various stages of its development, Michael Grabski, who translated the Swedish book into German and who suggested a number of changes, many of which have been incorporated into the present version, and John Lyons, an editor of this series. We are also grateful to Peter Hinst for a devastating review of the German version in *Zeitschrift für Germanistische Linguistik*, 3: 3 (1975), with which we partly agree. Were it not for our stubbornness, all these people might have managed to exert a still more positive influence on this book. For kind assistance with typing and editorial matters, we want to thank Pierre Javanaud, Ann-Mari Ranstrand and the staff of the Cambridge University Press.

Although the book is the result of team-work, the main responsibility for the respective chapters has been distributed as follows: chapters 1, 3, 4, 8 and 9.3 – Jens Allwood; chapters 5 and 6 – Lars-Gunnar Andersson; and chapters 2, 7, 10 and the rest of chapter 9 – Östen Dahl.

Symbols and notational conventions

Symbol	Name		Explained
∈	element sign ('is a member of')	*page*	3
∉	'is not a member of'		3
{ }	curly brackets (denoting sets)		3–4
∅	empty set		4
1	universal set		5
⊂	proper inclusion ('is a proper subset of')		6
⊆	inclusion ('is a subset of')		6
=	set identity		6
∩	intersection		7
∪	union		7
−	difference		8
C	complement		9
⟨⟩	angle brackets (denoting n-tuples)		9
t	'true'		28
f	'false'		28
|	Sheffer's stroke		29
∼ (¬, −)	negation		30
& (·, ∧)	conjunction		32
∨	disjunction (inclusive)		34
⊚	disjunction (exclusive)		35
→ (⊃)	implication (material)		37
≡ (↔, ⊇)	equivalence		41
∀	universal quantifier		62
∃	existential quantifier		65
Ř	converse of R		90
M (◇)	possibility operator		109
N (□)	necessity operator		109
⥽	strict implication ('fishhook')		111

Symbols

$\rightarrow\!\Box\!\rightarrow$	counterfactual operator	120
$F, H, G,$	tense operators	
A		121
ι	iota-operator	152
λ	lambda-operator	155
$A, B, C...$	(in set theory) sets	3
	(in predicate logic) predicate constants	59
$a, b, c...$	(in set theory) elements of sets	3
	(in predicate logic) individual constants	59
$\mathscr{A}, \mathscr{B}, \mathscr{C}...$	sets of sets	6
$f, g, h...$	functions	12
$p, q, r...$	sentential variables	26
$x, y, z...$	individual variables	59
$\Phi, \Psi, \mathsf{X}...$	predicate variables	59
$\alpha, \beta, \gamma...$	metavariables for wffs	71
$P, Q, R...$	metavariables for predicate terms	71
$t_1, t_2...t_n$	metavariables for individual terms	71

Expressions in English and other natural languages are quoted in italics, e.g. *horse*, when what is referred to is the expression itself, and between quotes, e.g. 'horse', when what is referred to is the meaning of the expression.

When an important term is introduced, it is given in bold type, e.g. **extension**.

I

Logic for linguists

Most twentieth-century linguists have regarded the structural aspects of language as their main object of study. This applies not only to those linguists usually referred to as structuralists (e.g. Saussure, Hjelmslev, Bloomfield and the Prague school), but perhaps even more to Chomsky and the generative transformational school, which made important breakthroughs in the formal study of linguistic structure.[1] But the most striking successes of structuralism have been in the fields of phonology, morphology and syntax. When it comes to the formal structure of the content or meaning of language there is much less agreed progress. Many structuralists have actually chosen to disregard the content of language, even to the point of denying that semantics is a part of linguistics.

Thus some of the most interesting attempts to characterize the structure of the content as well as structure in general are to be found not within linguistics proper but within formal logic. Although twentieth-century logic has concentrated on the logic of mathematics and mathematical language, ordinary everyday language has also been analysed, though less thoroughly, by logicians such as Frege, Russell, Carnap, Reichenbach and Montague.[2] Linguists and logicians have now begun seriously to apply logical methods to the study of natural languages, and several very interesting analyses of semantic structure have appeared.

The purpose of this introduction is to present linguistics students and others who are interested in the semantics of natural languages with some of the basic logical concepts and theories. Some knowledge of these is now necessary for anyone studying contemporary semantics or, for that matter, linguistics generally. Methods developed within formal logic to study the semantics of artificial languages have been fruitfully

---

[1] For a brief account of structural linguistics, see Davies (1973).
[2] For a history of ancient and modern logic, see Kneale and Kneale (1962).

applied to the semantics of natural language; and within linguistic theory in general, methods and approaches taken from logical and mathematical theory have become increasingly common. The 'phrase-structure' grammar that was presented by Chomsky in *Syntactic Structures* (1957) is a good example of this. Chomsky was here able to apply 'rewrite systems' to natural language, using a kind of grammar developed by the American logician Post to describe the structure of formal languages.[3]

We also want to help bridge the gap between linguistics and logic and thus to encourage closer cooperation between logicians and linguists in their common study of the structure of language. Although the introductory and pedagogical aspects of this book are the most important, we want to try also to substantiate our claim that logic is an area worth studying for those primarily concerned with natural language by providing examples of how logical analysis can be applied to natural language, and by discussing the relationship between logical and linguistic analysis and between logic and natural language. Some of the ideas we will present are comparatively new.

The whole book can be seen as an implicit argument for the relevance of logic to linguistics. In the final chapter there is an explicit discussion of this question.

[3] Post (1936).

2
Set theory

2.1. Sets and elements

In the following chapters, we shall often use concepts taken from **set theory**.[1] In addition to its connections with logic, set theory is fundamental to mathematics and has a number of direct applications in linguistics. We shall therefore start by characterizing briefly the most important concepts in this field.

A **set** is a number or collection of things or entities of any kind. Other terms that are often used to refer to sets are 'class' and 'group' (although these also have other, technical uses in mathematics). A set consists of a number of **elements** or **members**. The sets we have occasion to talk about in everyday life usually consist of elements that have something in common, such as the set of all Swedes or the set of all books in a certain library. Set theory puts no such restriction on sets: a set can be formed out of elements that have no connection whatsoever. We might for instance choose to consider the set which consists of the Premier of Sweden, the smallest moon of Mars and the square root of 7.

Some notational conventions: we shall use italic capital letters (A, B, C...) to refer to sets and italic lower-case letters (a, b, c...) to refer to the individual objects that are members of the sets. We introduce a special symbol, $\in$, to be read 'is an element of' or 'is a member of'. For instance, 'a is a member of B' is written $a \in B$. If we wish to say that a is not a member of B, we write $a \notin B$.

We also need a notation for writing expressions such as 'the set which consists of the following individuals: John, Bill, Harry' or 'the set of all Englishmen who have red hair'. We do this by using curly brackets, { }. As can be seen by the examples we gave, there are at least two ways to

---

[1] Good introductions to set theory are e.g. Halmos (1960), Lipschutz (1964) and Stoll (1961).

3

define sets: by **enumeration** and by **description**. With curly brackets, our examples will look as follows.

Enumeration: {John, Bill, Harry}
Description: $\{x|x$ is an Englishman with red hair} (to be read: 'the set of all x such that x is an Englishman with red hair')

There are also everyday constructions to express the same thing. Enumerations are usually formed with the conjunction *and*, e.g. *John (and) Bill and Harry*, and for descriptions we use relative clauses, e.g. *those who are Englishmen*.

Although this may astonish some people, set theory allows sets where the number of elements is one or zero. For each individual or object in the world, there is a set which has as its only member that individual or that object. For instance, given a person a, we can form a set $\{a\}$. It is important to remember that a and $\{a\}$ are different things – a is not a set.

A set with only one member is called a **unit set**. A set which has no (zero) members is called an **empty set**, or rather, the empty set, since there is only one such set, with the special symbol ø. The reason for this is that there is a general principle in set theory which is called the **principle of extensionality** and which says the following: for two sets to be distinct from each other, there must be at least one thing that is an element of one of them and not of the other. In other words, if the list of elements is the same, we are dealing with the same set. Any empty set will obviously have the same list of members, so there is only one empty set. A slightly paradoxical consequence of this is that e.g. the set of all female Presidents of the United States is identical to the set of all dogs that can write computer programs. However, we understand this better if we contemplate the difference between (a) the way in which the elements of a set are chosen (the criteria for distinguishing between elements and non-elements) and (b) the elements that are actually chosen. Obviously, the same elements may be chosen in many different ways. The idea of the principle of extensionality is that one entirely disregards the ways in which the members of a set have been chosen. This is related to a distinction which will be of great importance in the following chapters, namely that between **intension** and **extension** of an expression in a language. Consider a noun-phrase which describes a set, e.g. *the Englishmen who have red hair*. We can say that this noun-phrase picks out (or refers to) certain entities or things in the world by specifying a number of properties that are common to them. The entities picked out or referred to – i.e. the individuals who are Englishmen and have red hair – constitute the extension of the noun-phrase, whereas the way in which they are picked out – i.e. the criteria used to determine the extension of the expression – would be the intension of the phrase. We now see that the concept of 'set' in set theory can be said to be **extensional** in the sense that one does not bother about the ways in which the members of a set have been chosen – hence the name of the principle of extensionality.

What we have said here also shows that the mathematical concept of a set is not quite identical to the everyday concept for which we use words such as 'class' and 'group', even if we assumed that this was the case at the beginning of this chapter. When we talk about groups, e.g. groups of people, in everyday life, we often think of them as being the same at different points in time, although their members change. Thus, we may talk about e.g. the group of people who govern Britain, even saying things such as *This group has more members than it used to have*, a sentence which would be contradictory if the principle of extensionality were supposed to hold for the entity referred to by *this group*. Notice also that whereas there are a great many things that can be said of groups, e.g. that they perform such-and-such (collective) actions (as in *Our group sent a petition to the Government*), at least some mathematicians would say that sets are abstract entities which cannot do such things.

Another special set is the **universal set,** which is symbolized as 1 (the number one). To explain the universal set, we have to introduce another notion: that of a **universe of discourse,** which can be loosely defined as 'everything that is talked about in a certain text or a certain conversation'. For instance, in a mathematical textbook, the universe of discourse might be all numbers, whereas in a textbook in physics it might be all physical bodies. The universal set will then be the set of all individuals in the relevant universe of discourse.

2.2. Relations between sets

A number of concepts in set theory concern relations between sets. These relations may be represented by drawing the sets as circles. Consider for instance the set of all Europeans and the set of all Englishmen. Since all Englishmen are Europeans, we may draw a diagram (1) to represent the relations between the two sets, where A is the set of all

(1)

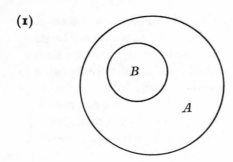

Europeans and B is the set of all Englishmen. In such a case, we say
that B is a subset of A or that B is included in A. In set theory, two
relations are usually distinguished: inclusion and proper inclusion. If
a set B is properly included in a set A, all members of B are members of
A and there is in addition at least one member of A that is not a member
of A. We then write $B \subset A$ with the symbol $\subset$ for 'is properly included in' or 'is a proper subset of'. If, as is often the case, we do not
want to make the claim that A contains at least one member that does
not belong to B, we write $B \subseteq A$, which is then simply 'B is included
in A' or 'B is a subset of A'.

If we want to say that A and B are the same set – in other words, that
they are identical – we write $A = B$. We saw in the preceding section
that this means that they have the same members.

It is important to distinguish between the relations 'is an element
(is a member) of' and 'is a subset of'. The set of all Englishmen is
a subset of the set of all Europeans, but it is not a member of it. John
Smith, on the other hand, is a member of the set of all Englishmen, but
he is not a subset of it.

2.3.   **Operations on sets**
There are also sets the members of which are other sets.
(Such sets are sometimes called **collections** or **families**.) For instance,
for any set, say A, we can form the set which consists of all subsets of A.
This set is called the **power set** of A. Example: The set $\{a, b\}$ has the
following subsets: $\{a\}$, $\{b\}$, $\{a, b\}$, $\varnothing$. (The empty set is a subset of all
sets.) The power set of $\{a, b\}$ is then $\{\{a\}, \{b\}, \{a, b\}, \varnothing\}$.

To distinguish sets of sets from ordinary sets, we may refer to them
by using capital script letters, e.g. $\mathcal{A}$.

We talked above about different ways of defining sets. A set can also be defined in terms of other sets by using so-called **set operations** or **operations on sets**. Given two sets A and B, we may define the set that consists of all objects that are members of both A and B. This set is called the **intersection** of A and B and is denoted by $A \cap B$. In (1), it corresponds to the shaded area.

(**1**)

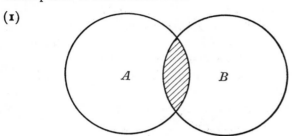

Example: If A is the set of all linguists and B is the set of all Swedes, then $A \cap B$ is the set of all Swedish linguists.

We may also want to talk about the set of all objects that are members of either of the sets A and B. This set is called the **union** of A and B and is denoted by $A \cup B$. It is shown in (2).

(**2**)

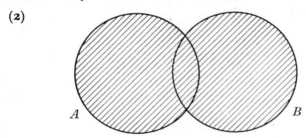

Example: If A is the set of all people who have read *War and Peace* and B is the set of all people who have read *Anna Karenina*, then $A \cup B$ is the set of all people who have read *War and Peace* or *Anna Karenina* (or both).

(**3**)

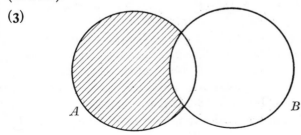

The shaded set, i.e. the set of all objects that are members of A but not members of B, is called the **difference** of A and B and is denoted by $A-B$ (read 'A minus B'). Example: If A is the set of all Englishmen and B is the set of all people who can talk Portuguese, then $A-B$ is the set of all Englishmen who cannot talk Portuguese (all Englishmen except those who can talk Portuguese).

So far, we have only talked about operations on pairs of sets. There is nothing, however, to prevent us from extending the operations to apply to three or more sets. For instance, we could define the intersection of A, B, C, D (the set which contains all objects which are members of all the four sets A, B, C and D) to be an operation on the set of sets $\{A, B, C, D\}$ which can be denoted by $\cap \{A, B, C, D\}$ (the shaded area in (4)).

(4)

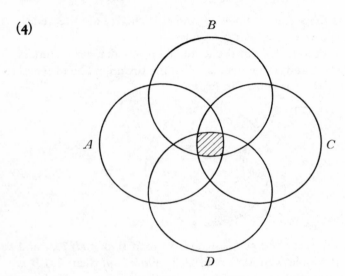

In the same way, the union of A, B, C and D (the set which contains all objects which are members of at least one of the four sets A, B, C and D) can be denoted by $\cup \{A, B, C, D\}$ (the shaded area in (5)).

A further important concept is that of the **complement** of a set. Given a certain universe of discourse U, e.g. the set of all human beings, and a subset A of that set, e.g. the set of all Frenchmen, then we can also talk about the set of all members of U which are not members of A, i.e. in this case the set of all humans that are not Frenchmen. This set is then called the **complement** of A with respect to U. In (6) the rectangle

(5)

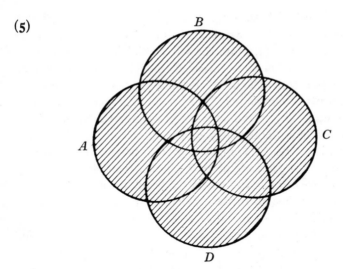

is U, the circle is the set A and the shaded area the complement of A, which is symbolized as CA or A^-.

(6)

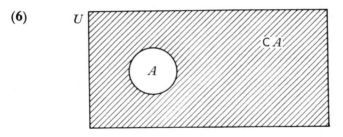

2.4. **Relations and functions**

A set of two elements is called a **pair**. If we decide to regard the elements of the pair as ordered in some way, we obtain an **ordered pair**. To denote ordered pairs, we use angle brackets $\langle\ \rangle$ instead of curly brackets $\{\ \}$. (Sometimes ordinary parentheses ( ) are used.)[2]

---

[2] Although this is the way that the concept of an ordered pair is introduced in most textbooks (e.g. those mentioned in n. 1 above), it is not quite correct. As is pointed out in the main text, the concept of an ordered pair is used to explicate the concept of a two-place relation. Consider the case when someone or something stands in a certain relation to himself or itself, e.g. the case of Oedipus, who was his own stepfather. Which ordered pair does this relation correspond to? The only possible answer is the one designated by $\langle$Oedipus, Oedipus$\rangle$. But this is no set of two elements, since the first element is identical to the second. So what we

9

When we are dealing with unordered sets, the order in which we enumerate the elements has no significance. Thus $\{a, b\}$ is the same set as $\{b, a\}$. The ordered pair $\langle a, b \rangle$ on the other hand, is not identical to the ordered pair $\langle b, a \rangle$. To make this clear, we shall here briefly consider the concept of a **relation**, which will be discussed in more detail in section 5.8. A two-place relation, e.g. 'to be more intelligent than' holds between two individual objects, which must be regarded as the members of an ordered pair. It is immediately clear that the order of the two individual objects is essential: 'Hengist is more intelligent than Horsa' is not the same thing as 'Horsa is more intelligent than Hengist.'

In the same way, we can talk about ordered **triples** (with 3 elements), **quadruples** (4 elements), **quintuples** (5 elements) and generally about ordered n-**tuples**.(These correspond to 3-, 4-, 5- and n-place relations, respectively.) The days of a year can be regarded as an ordered 365-tuple.

A very important concept in logic, mathematics and linguistics is that of a **function**. Let us take an example. Every motor-car has a licence number. Consider now the set of all motor-cars and all licence numbers. We represent them in (1).

(1)

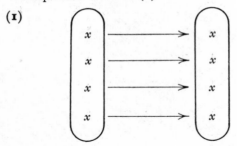

Each x represents an element in its respective set. (There should of course be many more elements.) From each element in the set to the

want instead is an abstract object which can be represented as something consisting of two 'slots', where the first member of the ordered pair goes into the first slot and the second goes into the second, but where the same entity can occupy both slots at once. The two possibilities can be illustrated by two 'games'. Imagine that we have before us a box with marbles. In both games, the player has to make two choices of a marble from the box, but in the second game he puts back the first marble he has chosen before he makes the second choice, so that he can choose it another time if he wants to. Only in the first case do we necessarily obtain a set of two members. We might thus distinguish – corresponding to the two games – two concepts; AN ORDERED SET WITH n MEMBERS and AN ORDERED n-TUPLE, where only the second allows for one element to occur at several places. An ordered pair is then an ordered 2-tuple.

left, i.e. the set of all motor-cars, there is an arrow to an element in the set to the right, viz. to the licence number that belongs to that car. In this way, we obtain a huge number of ordered pairs where the first element is a car and the second its licence number, e.g. ⟨John Smith's car, AAA 111⟩. To each element in the first set, we have **assigned** an element in the second set. Such an assignment is called a **function**. For there to be a function, there should be exactly one element in the second set for each element in the first set (it is possible for several elements of the first set to share one element in the second set). In other words, the arrows may converge but must not diverge. (We shall return to this question when discussing formal properties of relations in section 5.8.)

Suppose now we have two sets A and B as in (2) and a function (symbolized by the arrow) which assigns an element of B to each element

(2)

of A. We then say that we have a **function from** A **into** B or a function which **maps** A **into** B. The latter locution may seem strange at first, but it is often used in technical linguistic literature. For example, a transformation in transformational grammar may be regarded as a function which maps a set of structures into another set of structures, which is a fancier way of saying that for each structure that 'enters' the transformation there is exactly one structure coming out of it.

More everyday examples of functions may be found for example in any book containing statistical tables. For instance, we may find a table listing the countries of Europe and their population (3).

(3)   Albania   2,337,600
           Andorra   25,000
           Austria   7,456,403
           . . .   . . .

Such a table represents a function where the left-hand column corresponds to the set A in (2) and the right-hand column to the set B. In other words, we have a function which maps the set of countries into the set of numbers.

There is more terminology to be explained. Each item in the left-hand column is an **argument** of the function, and the corresponding item in the right-hand column is the **value** of the function for that argument. The function itself is denoted by small letters starting with f, and when we write $f(x)$, we mean the value that the function has for the argument x. If f is the function represented in the table above, we can write e.g. f (Sweden) = 8,000,000, meaning that the function takes the value 8,000,000 for the argument Sweden – in other words that the population of Sweden is eight million.

The set of all possible arguments of a function (for instance, the set A in (2)) is called the **domain** of the function, whereas the set of all possible values of the function is called the **range** or **co-domain** of the function.

If every element of B is the value of the function for some element in A, we say that the function **maps** A **onto** B (rather than **into** B). If A and B are the same set, i.e. the function maps A onto itself, the function is said to be an **operation**. An example of an operation from mathematics is 'the cube of', which maps numbers onto numbers (e.g. the cube of 3 is 9). If the natural numbers from 1 to any arbitrary number n are mapped onto another set A of objects, we obtain a **sequence** (in effect, each member in A obtains one or more numbers). Some functions have more than one argument. Consider for instance a table of the distances in miles between the major cities of the world. It may look like (4).

(4)

	Berlin	Buenos Aires	Cairo	Calcutta
Berlin	—	7,402	1,795	4,368
Buenos Aires	7,402	—	7,345	10,265
Cairo	1,795	7,345	—	3,539
Calcutta	4,368	10,265	3,539	—

In this case, the function takes a pair of cities as arguments and a distance as value.

We shall conclude this chapter by mentioning a special type of function that will be of some use to us later. Let us consider two sets A and B such that B is a subset of A. A might for instance be the set of members of the British Parliament, and B the set of MPs who belong to the majority party. Take then a third set C which contains just two elements, for instance the set consisting of the number 1 and 0. We can now construct a function which to any member of A assigns 1 if it is also a member of B and 0 if it is not, i.e. if it is in the complement of

B relative to *A*. This function is called the **characteristic function** of the set *B* relative to the domain *A*.

The choice of the two-member set is in fact arbitrary: any pair of objects would do as long as they distinguished the members of the set we want to characterize from its complement. In logic, it is common to identify the truth-values 'true' and 'false' (which we shall return to in section 3.4) with the two arbitrary objects used as the range of the characteristic function.

EXERCISES

1. Express in symbols:
   (*a*) *b* is an element of *C*
   (*b*) *C* is a proper subset of *D*
   (*c*) the union of *A* and *C*
   (*d*) the set which consists of the elements *d, e* and *g*
   (*e*) *d* is not an element of the intersection of *A* and *B*
   (*f*) the complement of *A* is a proper subset of the union of *B* and *C*
2. Translate the following expressions into idiomatic English.
   (*a*) $\{x \mid x$ is a boy and Mary has kissed $x\}$
   (*b*) $\{x \mid x$ is a Dane$\} \cap \{x \mid x$ is a philosopher$\}$
3. What is the power set of {London, Edinburgh, Dublin}?
4. Consider the following diagram.

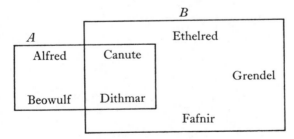

Which of the following statements are true and which are false?
   (*a*) Alfred is an element of $A \cup B$
   (*b*) Alfred is an element of $A \cap B$
   (*c*) $A \cap B$ has two elements
   (*d*) {Ethelred, Fafnir} $\subset$ $(A \cup B)$
   (*e*) {Ethelred, Fafnir, Grendel} $\subset$ $(B - A)$
   (*f*) {Ethelred, Fafnir, Grendel} $\subseteq$ $(B - A)$

5. Shade the area corresponding to the set C($A \cap B$).

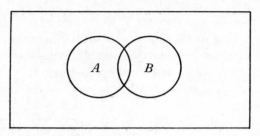

6. Which of the following statements are true and which are false?
   (*a*) $c \in \{a, b, c\}$
   (*b*) $d \notin \{a, b, c\}$
   (*c*) $\{a, b, c\} \subset \{a, b, c\}$
   (*d*) $\{a, b, c\} \subseteq \{a, b, c\}$
   (*e*) $\{a, b\} \subseteq \{a, b, c\}$
   (*f*) $c \in \{b, \{c\}\}$
   (*g*) $\{c\} \in \{b, \{c\}\}$
7. Find the domains and co-domains of the following functions.
   (*a*) 'the capital (city) of'
   (*b*) 'the wife of' (in a monogamous society)
   (*c*) 'the headmaster (or headmistress) of'

3
Inference and logical analysis of sentences[1]

3.1. **Inference**

Compare the following two arguments.[2]

(1)   All John's friends are my friends
        All my friends are nice
        Therefore all John's friends are nice
(2)   None of John's friends are my friends
        None of John's friends are nice
        Therefore none of my friends are nice

We immediately notice the difference between (1) and (2): if we reason as in (1), we think correctly, and if we reason as in (2), we think incorrectly. We will say that in (1) the **conclusion** (the sentence beginning with *therefore*) follows from the **premises** (the sentences the argument uses as a base, here the first two sentences of (1) and (2)). When a conclusion follows from its premises it is always the case that if the premises are true, then the conclusion will also be true. In (2), it is not certain that the conclusion would be true even if the premises were true. It could be, but this would not depend on its relation to the premises. In (1), however, we can be sure that if the premises are true the conclusion is also true. (1) is therefore a **logically valid inference**.

---

[1] The material covered in chapters 3–5 is treated in a large number of textbooks, some of which are Carnap (1958), Reichenbach (1966), Resnik (1970), Strawson (1967), Tarski (1965) and Thomason (1970), all of which can be recommended. Reichenbach and Strawson are the most linguistically oriented of those. Slightly more advanced are Anderson and Johnstone (1962), van Fraassen (1971), Mates (1965) and Mendelson (1964).

[2] 'Argument' is here used in the ordinary sense of reasons supporting a conclusion and not in the technical sense of input to a function as introduced in chapter 2.

One of the most important aspects of logic is the study of valid inferences and sentences that are necessarily true. There are two main types of inference: those that are necessarily valid and those that are valid only with a greater or lesser degree of probability.

Each type of inference is correlated with a special type of logical study. The study of necessarily valid inferences is pursued within **deductive logic,** while inferences that are valid with some degree of probability are studied within **inductive logic.** Consider the following two examples, which illustrate the difference between a deductive and an inductive inference.

(3)   DEDUCTIVE INFERENCE

    Premises: If it's snowing it's cold
                  It is snowing

    Conclusion: It is cold

(4)   INDUCTIVE INFERENCE

    Premises: When it's snowing it's usually cold
                  It is snowing

    Conclusion: It is cold

We can see that the conclusion of the inductive inference is valid only with a certain probability and is not necessarily valid as in the deductive inference.

Deductive logic has so far been more thoroughly investigated than inductive logic. Since it is furthermore the case that deductive logic provides the most interesting insights into the structure of language, we will in what follows deal only with deductive logic. We will from now on use the term 'logic' to be synonymous with deductive logic.

Logic will thus be the study of those properties that make an inference necessarily valid or a sentence necessarily true. Since valid inferences are inferences where the conclusion is logically entailed by the premises, interest in logic is focused on the study of **logical entailment** or **consequence.**

Logical validity and logical truth are in a certain sense completely independent of the factual validity or truth of what is stated or argued for. Logical validity and truth are also independent of the nature of the subject area the statements or arguments refer to. To understand what we mean by this, we will consider some examples of inferences.

(5)   Premises: Either the Anarchists or the Communists will
                     win the final victory
                     The Communists won't
        _____
        Conclusion: The Anarchists will win the final victory

Notice that the validity of this argument is not dependent on its being about Anarchists and Communists and who will win the final victory. We can see that the following argument is of the same type and valid in the same way.

(6)   Premises: Either Columbus or Leif Eriksson discovered
                     America first
                     Columbus did not
        _____
        Conclusion: Leif Eriksson discovered America first

The properties which are common to the arguments (5) and (6) and which make them valid we call the **logical form** of the arguments. We will consider this concept more closely in the next section.

In order to illustrate the point that the validity of an argument is totally independent of the factual truth of its premises and conclusion, we will consider three more arguments.

(7)   Premise: The owl and the fox are both birds
        _____
        Conclusion: The owl is a bird

(7) is a valid inference, in spite of its premise being factually false and only its conclusion true.

(8)   Premises: If the moon is a piece of green cheese every-
                     body is happy
                     The moon is a piece of green cheese
        _____
        Conclusion: Everybody is happy

(8) is a valid inference, in spite of both its premises and conclusion probably being false.

If we try to combine a true premise with a false conclusion as in (9) we will find that the result cannot possibly be a valid inference.

(9)   Premise: All whales are mammals
        _____
        Conclusion: Whales are fish

Thus, logical inference is truth-preserving; it tells us what has to be the case if the premises are true. In other words, if the premises of an argument happen to be true the conclusion must also be true. Since logical validity and truth can be said to be independent of factual truth, they are often, instead, said to be dependent on the form (structure) and meaning of those sentences that appear in the arguments which are studied. Logic disregards the question whether what has been said is really true, in order to concentrate on what has to true if the premises are true. The factual truth of premises and conclusion is not a logical problem, However, if the premises happen to be true, the conclusions we draw from them will naturally be true.

Logical validity and truth are formal, something which is often interpreted to mean that logical validity and truth depend on the form (structure) of a sentence or an argument rather than on what it is about. Because of this, logical inferences (truths) can be said to be valid (true) independently of what the world is like.

3.2. **Logical form**

Let us now consider some examples where an argument is expressed by one sentence.

(1)   All humans are mortal; therefore some humans are mortal

(2)   All swans are white; therefore some swans are white

(3)   Not all humans are wise; therefore some humans are not wise

(4)   Not all swans are white; therefore some swans are not white

We again see that it is the logical form of the sentences, and not what they are about, which decides the validity of the argument. We cannot trace the validity to the factual truth of the sentences concerned. The argument in (2) is valid in spite of the fact that all swans in reality are not white. There are also black swans. The validity of the argument is dependent only on the fact that the conclusion would have to be the case if the premises were true.

One could say that the logical form of the premises decides what is true (what conclusions can be drawn) if we assume that the premises are true. An argument is valid when the logical form or the premises really has the conclusion as a consequence. What the premises are about is immaterial. They can be factually true or false. In logic we are interested only in whether the truth of the premises really entails the truth of the conclusion and we completely disregard the question of what is really the case.

We will now study how one can say that logical validity depends on certain formal relations between sentences and sentential components. These formal relations are usually dependent on the occurrence of certain logical words or particles. In our four examples above these logical particles are *all*, *some* and *not*. We can now write the four examples in the following way.

(1) and (2) All *S* are *P*; therefore some *S* are *P*
(3) and (4) Not all *S* are *P*; therefore some *S* are not *P*

The logical form of the four arguments has now become more perspicuous and we can more easily see the formal relations that make the arguments valid.

An important principle in logic, which we can now express, is (5).

(5)   If an argument or a sentence of a certain logical form is logically valid or true then all arguments and sentences of the same logical form are valid and true respectively.

A warning is in order here: logical form is not the same as what in traditional grammar has been called grammatical form. In fact it is a very difficult problem to determine exactly how grammatical form and logical form correspond. As we shall see later in this book, many theories about the relationship between logical form and grammatical form have been proposed in the last few years. It has for example been suggested that logical form could be equated with concepts found within the various versions of transformational grammar like 'deep structure', 'conceptual structure' or 'semantic representation'.

We can easily see that it is insufficient to take only the superficial grammatical structure into account when drawing logical conclusions. Consider the following two sentences.

(6)   Richard is a one-eyed murderer
(7)   Richard is a supposed murderer

Although (6) and (7) have very similar surface structures, the conclusion expressed in (8) can be drawn only from (6).

(8)   Richard is a murderer

Since the concept of logical form (structure) is so important in logic – we have seen that it is the form that determines logical validity and truth – one of the most important tasks in logic is to characterize as precisely and clearly as possible just what logical form is. A way of doing this is to find a manner of expression or a **notation** which mirrors the logical form of a sentence and the logical relations that can hold between the logical forms of sentences.

3.3. **Sentences and propositions**

We have said that logic concerns itself with inferences, that is to say, how one proceeds from premises to conclusions. When we introduced the concepts of premise and conclusion, we spoke of them as if they referred to sentences. It has therefore seemed as though logic studies the relations between sentences. This is not completely true, at least not if by 'sentence' one means a certain sequence of sounds or letters. Consider sentence (1) once more.

(1)   All John's friends are my friends

If we heard this sentence uttered, is it clear that we could draw any conclusions about particular individuals from it?

No; first we must know who has uttered it, as we would otherwise not know who *my* referred to. To know what inferences are possible from a certain sentence, we must first know what the sentence says about the world. The same sentence uttered by different persons or at different times can say very different things about the world. If for example Josephine, speaking about Napoleon, at 2 p.m. on 6 January 1806 said, '*He is hungry now*', she would have said something quite different from what Krupskaya would have said if she had uttered the same sentence, referring to Lenin, at 3 p.m. on 7 January 1920. One of the sentences would be a statement about Napoleon, while the other would be a statement about Lenin.

What we are dealing with in an inference is what a sentence says about the world rather than the sentence as a sequence of sounds or signs. We will introduce the term **proposition**[3] to designate what a sentence says about the world.

As we have already seen, the same sentence can express different propositions on different occasions. Conversely, different sentences can

---

[3] A caveat is in order, since the term 'proposition' is used in several other ways in linguistics and logic.

express one and the same proposition. The sentence *It's Monday today* uttered on a Monday expresses the same proposition as *It was Monday yesterday* uttered on a Tuesday.

If we want to indicate a proposition in ordinary language we often use a *that*-clause. The traditional distinction between direct and indirect speech can thus, in somewhat simplified terms, be said to be a distinction between talking about sentences and talking about propositions. Compare (2) and (3).

(2) John Lackland said, 'Taxes are good for peasants'
(3) John Lackland said THAT taxes were good for peasants

(2) is true only if John Lackland used the words *Taxes are good for peasants*. (3) is true if he expressed the content of the *that*-clause *that taxes were good for peasants*. He could have used other words or even another language:

(4) Skatter är bra för bönder
(5) It is beneficial for the peasantry to be taxed

In (3), where we have indirect speech, we are therefore saying that John Lackland asserted a certain proposition rather than a sentence.

Ordinary language gives some support to the view that propositions are what occur in inferences. It is more natural to use expressions such as *true* and *imply* about *that*-clauses than about directly quoted sentences. Below, the (a)-sentences are preferable to the (b)-sentences.

(6) (a) It is true that snow is white
    (b) 'Snow is white' is true
(7) (a) That snow is white implies that snow is not black
    (b) 'Snow is white' implies 'snow is not black'

Instead of 'proposition' we could have used the word **statement**, which often means proposition in ordinary language. The drawback in using 'statement' is that this seems to imply somebody's stating – somebody's uttering the statement.

It is common in logic to disregard the complicated relations between sentences and propositions and to pretend that each sentence corresponds exactly to one proposition and vice versa. Certain logicians – e.g. W. V. O. Quine – even think that the proposition is a superfluous entity. As a matter of fact, it is to some extent possible to get along without the distinction between sentences and propositions as long as one avoids such expressions as personal pronouns (*I, you, he*) and temporal adverbs like *today, now, yesterday,* the interpretation of which is dependent on the speech situation (see further, p. 121). One can then use the terms 'sentence' and 'proposition' without distinguishing them. We shall in what follows continue this practice, but the reader should always keep the distinction at the back of his mind.

3.4. Possible worlds and the truth-set of a proposition

Using set theory we can interpret the concept of a proposition formally. In order to do this we introduce the concept **possible world**. (In everyday conversation we often use words such as **case** or **situation** instead of 'world'.)

The idea is roughly this: we can all imagine that the world we live in could be somewhat different from what it in reality is, and we also seem to be able to talk meaningfully about what would happen if the world were different, as in the following sentence.

(1)   If it had not rained this morning, we would have gone to the country

We can thus say that there are several 'ways in which the world could have been'. Instead of this complex expression we will use the shorter expression 'possible world'.[4]

We have already said that a proposition is what a sentence on a certain occasion says about the world. We can express this in a different way. Let us say that a certain proposition, for example that Lincoln admired Jefferson Davis, is true. This is the same as saying that our world is one of a set of possible worlds, namely those worlds in which it holds that Lincoln admired Jefferson Davis. For every proposition we can find a set of possible worlds in which the proposition is true. We will call this set the **truth-set** of the proposition. One way to characterize a proposition is therefore to give its truth-set, i.e. the set of possible worlds in which it is true.

Correspondingly a possible world can be characterized as the set of propositions which are true in it (and thus describe it).

Another way of expressing the same idea is to talk about the characteristic function (see p. 13) of the truth-set instead of about the truth-set itself. We then obtain a function that assigns to each possible world

---

[4] 'Possible worlds' were introduced by G. W. v. Leibniz in his *Discourse on Metaphysics*. Leibniz held that our world is the best of all possible worlds. For a discussion of this idea, see Voltaire (1759).

one of the values 'true' and 'false', according as the proposition is true or false in that particular world. Indeed, some logicians identify the proposition with this function. Thus you will sometimes find statements to the effect that 'propositions are functions from possible worlds to truth-values'. Perhaps some kind of parable will make it easier to grasp this idea. Think of the proposition as a condition which is put on possible worlds. Imagine a supernatural being having all possible worlds in a great bag, then taking them out one by one and sorting them according to whether they conform to the condition or not (i.e. whether the proposition is true in that world or not) or rather putting a stamp 'true' or 'false' on them in the way a government inspector puts 'approved' or 'not approved' on goods, according as they conform to the regulations or not. Thus a proposition would be a principle for sorting worlds into two categories: those where the proposition is true and those where it is false. In this sense, a proposition is – or perhaps better – corresponds to a function from possible worlds to truth-values.

3.5. Analytic and synthetic sentences

Analytic truth is often introduced as a superordinate concept to logical truth. All logical truths are analytic, but there are analytic truths that are not logical. Those analytic truths that are logical truths, e.g.

(**1**)   It's not the case that water both is and is not a chemical element

are thought to be true because of their logical form, while other analytic truths depend on certain semantic relations between words that do not belong to the 'logical' vocabulary of the sentence or argument. **Synonymy** (identity or similarity of meaning) and **hyponymy** (inclusion of meaning) are the most common such semantic relations.[5] (2) below is an example of a sentence that because of partial synonymy is analytically true but not logically true.

(**2**)   All bachelors are unmarried

(3) below is an inference which is analytically valid because of hyponymy but not logically valid.

(**3**)   Premise: This is a rose

Conclusion: This is a flower

[5] See Lyons (1968) and Katz (1972) for a discussion of relations such as these.

The difference between those analytic truths that depend on logical form and those that depend on semantic relations is a difference of degree rather than category. Partly, the choice between what one wants to call form (or structure) and what one wants to call meaning in a sentence is arbitrary. In the last instance it is a matter of decision whether a word belongs to the logical vocabulary or not.

If one negates an analytically true sentence, one gets a sentence that because of its form or meaning must be false – an **analytically false** sentence or a contradiction, e.g. (4).

(4)   It is not true that all bachelors are unmarried

Analytically true and analytically false sentences can both be called **analytic sentences**.[6] They have in common that their truth is independent of what the world looks like. An analytically true sentence is TRUE IN ALL POSSIBLE WORLDS; an analytically false sentence is FALSE IN ALL POSSIBLE WORLDS. We can say that the truth-set of the analytically true sentences is 1 (the set of all possible worlds) and that that of the analytically false sentences is ø (the empty set).

Sentences that are not analytic are called **synthetic**. They are true or false depending on the appearance of the world – in other words, they are true in certain worlds and false in others. An example of a synthetic sentence is

(5)   Charles I was beheaded in 1649

Just as the boundary between logical and analytic truth is, to some extent, arbitrary, there is no hard-and-fast boundary between analytic and synthetic sentences. Is (6) analytic?

(6)   John's car has colour

It seems that in our world all material objects must have colour. Is this true in all possible worlds? So far we have no good answers to such questions; we are still waiting for a theory which in a principled way relates and distinguishes between synthetic, analytic and logically true sentences.

3.6.   **Simple and compound sentences**

An important trait of the traditional conception of logical structure is the idea that all sentences can be reduced to simple or

---

[6] Sometimes the term 'analytic sentence' is restricted to those sentences that are analytically true.

atomic sentences. These simple sentences are then combined or related to each other in various ways to form **compound** or **molecular** sentences. Every sentence is either simple or compound, that is, constructed from simple sentences in a definite way.

The distinction between simple and compound sentences is not new and not peculiar to logic. It also exists in traditional grammar, where the syntactic dependencies between simple sentences have long been studied under the headings 'coordination' and 'subordination' (parataxis and hypotaxis). (1) shows how by using *and* one can combine two simple sentences to form a compound sentence.

(1)

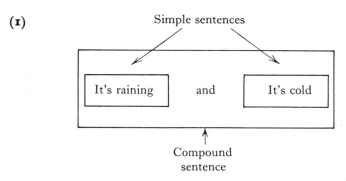

3.7. **The depth of the logical analysis**

The analysis of logical form can be carried on at different levels or with different degrees of fineness. A traditional way of dividing logic splits logic according to the level of refinement at which the analysis is carried out.

The shallowest or coarsest type of logical analysis is the one where one investigates the logical relations that hold between simple and compound sentences only and where the analysis of the internal logical structure of simple sentences is completely excluded. Simple sentences are taken as unanalysed wholes and we pay attention only to the way in which they are related to eath other.

The study of inter-sentential relations as distinguished from intra-sentential relations is carried on in **sentential** or **propositional logic**. If we also take the internal structure of simple sentences into account, we get **predicate logic** (see chapter 5) and various types of modal logic (see chapter 7).

4

Propositional logic

4.1. Connectives

Logical relations between simple sentences that are part of a compound sentence are usually determined by certain words called **sentential** (or **propositional**) **connectives**. A sentential connective is a word or phrase usually belonging to the traditional grammatical category of conjunction (*and, or, therefore, because, since, but, before, as, even though* and *if...then*).

In the following examples it is clear that the connectives combine sentences in logically distinct ways.

(1)   Bill is a syndicalist even though he reads Burke
(2)   Bill is a syndicalist and he reads Burke
(3)   Bill is a syndicalist or he reads Burke

In all three cases two sentences are combined, but with different effects depending on the connective chosen.

That we are really dealing with different logical relations can best be seen from the conclusions we can draw from the three sentences. From (1) it follows roughly that one does not expect a syndicalist to read Burke. From (2) and (3) no such conclusion can be drawn. (3) does not even imply that both sentences are true but only that at least one of them is true.

The logical form provided by the sentential connectives therefore determines the logical consequences of the sentences that have been related by the connectives.

Since we are not interested in the internal structure of sentences in propositional logic but only in the logical relations between sentences, we introduce so-called **sentential** (or **propositional**) **variables**, that is, signs that can stand for any declarative sentence. As variables, lower-case italic letters from p onwards are usually chosen. Using sentential variables, our three examples from above would appear as follows.

(**1′**)   *p* even though *q*
(**2′**)   *p* and *q*
(**3′**)   *p* or *q*

We are now using variables for the sentences but showing the logical structure with words. Whatever declarative sentences we let the variables represent, the logical structure will remain the same since it is dependent only on properties of the connectives and not on the content of the simple sentences.

In logic, signs that have a permanent non-variable meaning are called **constants**. Since the sentential connectives have this property and since they also are part of what we have called the logical vocabulary, they are called **logical constants,** i.e. signs that through their permanent meanings and functions determine the logical structure of the sentences they occur in. The variables are there to represent the content that is being structured, but the constants represent the structure itself. Besides sentential connectives such things as quantifiers and modal operators (which we will study below) are commonly counted as logical constants.

In propositional logic interest has traditionally been shown in only four of the sentential connectives of ordinary language, namely the four connectives *and, or, if...then* and *if and only if* (if the latter can be regarded as an ordinary language connective). There has also been study of how negation (*not*) affects sentences.

Most of the connectives of ordinary language have not been studied. Words like *therefore, since, while, although* and *before* have hardly been studied at all as far as their contribution to the logical structure of sentences is concerned.

There are two reasons for this. The first and perhaps most important is that logic has so far been studied primarily for its mathematical interest, which has led to a concentration on those types of inference which are common in mathematical reasoning. Many of the types of reasoning for which we use ordinary language are therefore relatively little explored.

The other reason is more serious from a theoretical point of view. It concerns the extent to which the connectives of natural language are **truth-functional**. To understand this question, we have to introduce the term **truth-value**. Every declarative sentence has one and only one truth-value. A true sentence has the truth-value 'true', while a false sentence has the truth-value 'false'. We abbreviate the two truth-values **t** and **f** respectively. Now consider the following example.

(**4**)   It is warm and windy

(4) can be paraphrased in a logically more transparent manner as

(**4′**)   It is warm and it is windy

For the compound expression (4′) to be true both (5) (a) and (5) (b) must be true.

(**5**) (a)   It is warm
    (b)   It is windy

Only when both the simple sentences that are combined by *and* are true is the compound sentence true. If one of the sentences or both are false, the compound expression is false. We can therefore say that the truth-value of the compound expression is a function of the truth-values of the simple sentences.

A connective which has the property of making the truth-value of the compound expression it creates computable from the truth-values of the simple sentences it connects is truth-functional. We can express this somewhat differently with the help of the following two sentential schemas.

(**6**) (a)   ——— and ———
    (b)   ——— or ———

Instead of variables we are using lines. *And* and *or* are both truth-functional and therefore the truth-values for those compound sentences that they create are completely determined by the truth-values of the sentences that could replace the lines.

One of the most important tasks of logic has traditionally been to show what correct conclusions can be drawn from a set of premises, or, in another formulation, what conclusions preserve the truth of the premises. It is therefore of great importance to understand the truth-functional properties of the connectives. These properties are what enable us to judge the validity of an argument, that is, to the extent that this is independent of the factual truth of the simple sentences.

Not all connectives are truth-functional. Consider, first, the differences between the following sentences.

(7)   There is a thunderstorm and I feel good
(8)   There is a thunderstorm but I feel good
(9)   Since there is a thunderstorm, I feel good

Both *and* and *since* require that the simple sentences they combine are true for the compound expression they create to be true. If this condition is met, the sentence with *and* is true, but not the sentence with *since*. This sentence can still be false. Over and above the truth-functional connection between the two simple sentences, *since* requires that one of them be a reason for the other. That is, it is necessary but not sufficient that the two simple sentences are true for the compound sentence with *since* to be true. *Since* is therefore not a truth-functional connective.

If we turn to *and* and *but*, the sentence with *but* is true if the two simple sentences it combines are true. So *but* is truth-functional. However, there still remains a difference between *and* and *but*, but the difference is not truth-functional and in logic as it has been developed so far, there is no method of treating it. All formal relations between sentences that are treated in propositional logic are truth-functional.

As we have seen, traditional propositional logic is limited by two factors: only truth-functional connectives have been studied, and among these only those that are relevant to mathematics have been studied systematically. To introduce more truth-functional connectives is considered trivial by the logician, as the rather small number of truth-functions is known and furthermore can be reduced to combinations of operations with one single function, namely the so-called Sheffer's stroke, which is written | ($p|q$ is read 'not both p and q').

Originally logic was conceived of as a tool to study the logical properties of natural language. By translating arguments in natural language into propositional calculus one hoped to obtain the arguments in a more perspicuous form, where it would be easier to see whether they were valid. However, the translation turned out to be difficult; natural language with its vagueness and ambiguity had to be transferred into a somewhat arbitrarily chosen unambiguous system of formal representation. Since such a system was considered a great advantage in other respects, logic became increasingly estranged from the study of natural language. We still have not discovered how best to study and formalize non-truth-functional relations between sentences, though the study of pragmatics, which we will touch on to some extent in chapter 9, perhaps provides one type of solution to this problem.

4.2. **The meaning of the logical connectives**

Let us now study somewhat more closely the meaning of the five connectives usually employed in propositional logic. The requirement that the connectives be truth-functional means that in logic they have a fixed and definite meaning which only partly covers their use in everyday language. In the following sections we will point out some of the differences between their meaning in ordinary language and in logic. The five connectives are: the **conjunction**[1] (*and*), the **disjunction** (*or*), the **implication** (*if...then*), the **equivalence** (*if and only if*) and the **negation** (*not*), which is not really a connective, since it does not combine sentences, but operates on one sentence at a time. All five are represented by special symbols in logic.

4.2.1. *Negation* ~

The following expressions commonly correspond to logical negation in ordinary language.

(**1**) (a) It is false that
   (b) It is not the case that
   (c) Not
   (d) It is incorrect that
   (e) It is not true that
   (f) It is wrong that

Negation is used in logic to form a compound sentence the truth-value of which is the opposite of that of the simple sentence it operates on. Thus, if *It's snowing* is true, *It's not snowing* must be false, and vice versa. In an abbreviated manner this can be expressed in the following way. We will use sentential variables and a special symbol for not, ~ ($\rightarrow$ and $-$ exist but are less common).

(**2**) p ~ p
       t   f
       f   t

An abbreviation of this type where the truth-values of ~ p (the complex sentence) are shown relative to the truth-values of p (the simple sentence) is called a **truth table**.

---

[1] The term 'conjunction' has a special use in logic and only designates *and*, while the traditional grammatical term 'conjunction' in logic more or less corresponds to the term 'connective'.

We can also characterize negation in terms of set theory. Consider (3). Let A be the truth-set for p, i.e. the set of all worlds where p is true. The truth-set for $\sim p$ will now be all worlds where p is false – which we can see is the same as C A, that is, the complement of A.

(3)

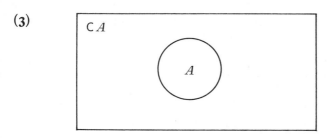

As we have mentioned, logical negation is not the exact equivalent of the expressions for negation in ordinary language. Ordinary language seems to allow negation below the sentence level, but this is not possible in propositional logic.

(4)   Non-students are not allowed

We would have to ignore the negative prefix *non-* and translate (4) as $\sim p$. Another difference is that the possibility of focusing different constituents in a negated sentence by stress and intonation is also lost in propositional logic. Compare (5) and (6).

(5)   Mary didn't kiss Bill
(6)   *Mary* didn't kiss Bill

(5), if spoken with normal stress and intonation, is the neutral negative of *Mary kissed Bill*, while (6), where *Mary* is stressed, seems to presuppose that someone else kissed Bill. The difference between (5) and (6) cannot be captured in propositional logic; both would be translated as $\sim p$.

(7)   Harold Bluetooth did not think Alfred was fond of cakes

Finally, (7) is ambiguous for many people, there being a choice between interpreting the subordinate or the main clause as negated. There is no hope of capturing any such complexity in the formal representation of propositional logic.

4.2.2. *Conjunction* &

The conjunction closely resembles *and* in everyday language. The conjunction is used in logic to construct a compound sentence which is true only if all the simple sentences (these are called **conjuncts**) from which it is constructed are true. If any simple sentence is false, the compound sentence or the **conjunction** (it is a general custom to use the name of the logical constant for the compound expression it creates) is also false. Thus (1) is true, while (2) is false.

(1)   George was mad and Pitt was Prime Minister

(2)   George was mad and Pitt was King

We can summarize this, too, in a truth table with sentential variables and a symbol for conjunction, &.

(3)

p	q	$p \ \& \ q$
t	t	t
t	f	f
f	t	f
f	f	f

We see that we have exhausted all the possibilities of combining the truth-values of p and q and that only if both conjuncts are true will the whole conjunction be true.

Let us now study the relation between the truth-set for $p \ \& \ q$ and the truth-set for the simple sentences it contains. In (4), A is the truth-set for p and B is the truth-set for q.

(4)

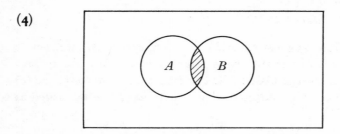

The truth-set for $p \ \& \ q$ is the set of all worlds where both p and q are true. This will be the same as the intersection between A and B. Generally it is true that the truth-set for a conjunction is equivalent to the intersection between the truth-sets of all the simple sentences that are part of the conjunction.

A different way of viewing the connection between conjunction and intersection can be illustrated in the following way. Let us suppose that Egbert (e) is a member of a chess club A and a soccer club B. Then it is true that $e \in A$ & $e \in B$. We know that a conjunction is true only if all the sentences from which the conjunction is constructed are true.

(5)

$e \in A$	&	$e \in B$
t	t	t
t	f	f
f	f	t
f	f	f

So only in the case where e is a member of both A and B, or in other words is a member of the intersection between A and B, will the complex conjunction of $e \in A$ and $e \in B$ be true.

Just as we observed with negation, the meaning of logical conjunction is somewhat different from *and* in everyday language. While & can only be used to combine sentences, *and* can be used to combine constituents below the sentence level as well. The *and* in *John and Bill* can receive no translation. Only if the terms that are combined can be distributed to different sentences is a translation to a compound sentence possible. (6) can be split into

(6)   John and Bill own a car

– two sentences (7) if John and Bill own a car each.

(7)   John owns a car and Bill owns a car   (p & q)

However, if they collectively own a car no such analysis is possible and p has to suffice as a translation.

Phrases combined with *and* in ordinary language often express sequences of events. If one changes the order of the conjuncts, the order of the events changes as well.

(8)   Gunnar lay down on the bed and died
(9)   Gunnar died and lay down on the bed

In logic p & q is always equivalent to q & p.[2] This makes logical conjunction atemporal and unable to handle the temporal aspects of *and*, which *and* can clearly be seen to possess if (8) is compared with (9).

----

[2] In mathematical terms, the conjunction is **commutative**, i.e.
$$p \ \& \ q \equiv q \ \& \ p.$$

There are many other uses of *and* in everyday language. Often these should not be analysed as logical conjunctions.

(**10**)   Touch me and I will kiss you
(**11**)   Run a mile every day and you will feel like a new man

(10) and (11) should probably be analysed as implications rather than conjunctions.

(**10**)(a)   *If* you touch me *then* I will kiss you
(**11**)(a)   *If* you run a mile every day *then* you will feel like a new man

In propositional logic it is common to admit only conjunctions of two sentences. In ordinary language there is no such limit, e.g.

(**12**)   Julius smokes and Octavian wenches and Anthony drinks and Cleo moans

There is nothing to prevent the construction of a propositional logic which works this way, i.e. letting the conjunction combine more than two sentences. It is then practical to put & in front of the sentences that are to be combined and write the expression in the following way: $\&\,(p, q, r, s, t, u, v, w)$. Naturally, this method of writing (so-called Polish notation, which we shall introduce in one of the exercises) can be used even if there are only two conjuncts. This will be true also of our next connective, the disjunction. Further, it should be noted that $((p \,\&\, q) \,\&\, r)$ is logically equivalent to $(p \,\&\, (q \,\&\, r))$, which means that a conjunction of any size can be reduced to a chain of binary conjunctions (in mathematical terminology we say that the conjunction is **associative**).

4.2.3.   *Disjunction* ∨

The disjunction most closely corresponds to *or* in ordinary language. The disjunction is used in logic to create a compound sentence (which is also called **disjunction**) which is false only if both the simple sentences (**disjuncts**) in it are false. It will therefore be enough that one disjunct is true for the whole disjunction to be true. Thus, given our present knowledge, (1) is false but (2) true.

(**1**)   Mars is a satellite or a black hole
(**2**)   Mars is a planet or a black hole

The truth table for the disjunction, with the special symbol ∨, is as follows.

(3)	p	q	$p \vee q$
	t	t	t
	t	f	t
	f	t	t
	f	f	f

We can see that a disjunction is false if both disjuncts are false; otherwise it is true.

In the preceding section we saw that conjunction corresponds to set-theoretical intersection. Let us now study the disjunction. A and B in (4) again correspond to the truth-sets for p and q respectively.

(4)

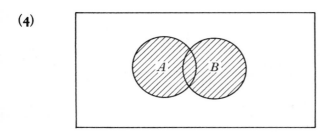

The truth-set for $p \vee q$ will be the set of all worlds where p or q is true – which is the same as the union of A and B. The truth-set for a disjunction is therefore equivalent to the union of the truth-sets of the simple sentences from which it is constructed.

We can also demonstrate the connection between conjunction and disjunction in a different way. Suppose that we know that Egbert (e) is a member of the chess club (A) or the soccer club (B) but we are not sure whether he is a member of both clubs or just one of them. The following will then be true: $e \in A \vee e \in B$. We see that the disjunction of the sentences $e \in A$ and $e \in B$ is true only if e is a member of the union of A and B.

Again there are discrepancies between logical disjunction and the use of *or* in ordinary language.

Often a stricter type of disjunction seems to be intended, a disjunction which would be true only if exactly one disjunct were true. This connective is sometimes given its own sign $\veebar$ and is called the **exclusive** disjunction in distinction to $\vee$, which is called **inclusive**. It has the following truth table.

35

(5)

p	q	$p \oslash q$
t	t	f
t	f	t
f	t	t
f	f	f

Here the disjunction will be false both when both disjuncts are true and when both disjuncts are false. Exclusive *or* is thus truth-functional but it is not the *or* that has primarily been chosen for representation in logic. One reason for this is that we can represent exclusive *or* using *and, not* and inclusive *or* in the following way.

(6) $\qquad (p \vee q) \ \& \sim (p \ \& \ q)$

Starting from inclusive *or*, we exclude the possibility that both p and q are true by negating the conjunction which says that both p and q are true. This is precisely the function of exclusive *or*. An *or* which seems to function exclusively can be found in *either...or* sentences, questions and requests.

(7) $\qquad$ Either God is good or he is not
(8) $\qquad$ Do you want red or white wine?
(9) $\qquad$ Your money or your life!

An *or* which has a more clearly inclusive character can be found in (10), where, of course, the common case will be for both disjuncts to be true of a person.

(10) $\qquad$ Everybody who is either a citizen of Sweden or has lived in Sweden during the past year is obliged to submit a tax return

It should also be pointed out that the air of uncertainty which in normal speech situations goes with a use of *or* is not required in logic. As far as logic is concerned, it is perfectly acceptable to utter the following sentence as one watches the first snow of winter falling.

(11) $\qquad$ It's snowing or raining

The only thing that is required of a disjunction for it to be true is the truth of one disjunct. This is the case even though it is totally precluded that it is raining. Normally, however, a lot more than truth-functional properties are involved in linguistic communication. The fact that (11) would be considered a very strange utterance in the situation we described shows that over and above truth-functional properties there are other factors which decide our interpretation of linguistic utterances. One suggestion for an analysis of these factors is to say that there is a set of communicative norms[3] which aim at making the exchange of information between the participants in a speech situation as effective as possible. Basing oneself on these norms one could say: one should not say $p \vee q$ if one can say p or $p \ \& \ q$, both of which by virtue of their truth-conditions give more definite information than $p \vee q$. One should utilize linguistic expressions as effectively as possible, making both what one says and what one does not say relevant to how what is said is understood. This is normally one of the implicit assumptions of linguistic communication.

4.2.4. *Implication* →

The implication of propositional logic is even more different from its corresponding expressions in ordinary language (*if...then, if* and, sometimes, *and*) than the other connectives we have discussed. Let us consider some examples of *if...(then)* in ordinary language.

(1)   If you have worked hard (then) you are probably tired
(2)   If it is raining (then) it will be wet
(3)   If Hengist is fatter than Horsa (then) Horsa is thinner than Hengist
(4)   If you are a good boy (then) you will get a cake

In (1) and (2), *if...then* expresses a 'causal tie' between the antecedent and consequent clause. In (4), the antecedent is tied to the consequent by a promissory obligation on the part of the speaker. In (3) we can say that a logical consequence has been expressed by *if...then*. In propositional logic the implication is treated only truth-functionally, and it has therefore simply been stipulated that an implication is true whenever its antecedent is false or its consequent true. The following truth table can then be given for implication. As special symbol, we introduce →. ($\supset$ is perhaps more common but is easily confused with $\subset$, the symbol for inclusion in set theory.)

---

[3] See Grice (1975) for an account of such norms.

(5)

p	q	$p \rightarrow q$
t	t	t
t	f	f
f	t	t
f	f	t

The truth-functional implication is usually called the **material implication** and, as we can see, it is only false if its antecedent is true and its consequent false. Let us see how this corresponds to the use of *if...then* in ordinary language.

One case seems relatively unproblematic: an *if...then* sentence as well as an $\rightarrow$ expression is false when its antecedent is true and its consequent false. Consider (6).

(6)   If London is the capital of England then England has no capital

Perhaps it also seems natural to say that the implication (the compound sentence) is true when both antecedent and consequent are true. Usually, however, more is required from a sentence constructed with *if...then* in ordinary conversation. It is usually required that the antecedent and consequent are tied together by some non-truth-functional tie like causality or logical consequence. See examples (1–4). Consider (7).

(7)   If Kennedy was a President then cabbage is a vegetable

Here antecedent and consequent are completely unrelated but both are true, and since the truth-values are the only relevant consideration in a truth-functional evaluation of a complex sentence, (7) must be treated in exactly the same way as other sentences with *if...then*, where besides both antecedent and consequent being true, there is some kind of non-truth-functional tie between them.

The situation becomes worse when the antecedent of an implication is false. One can consider a bet.

(8)   If it rains tomorrow I bet you there will be no excursion

If the condition about rain is not fulfilled the bet loses its force. It seems natural to think that this holds also for pure statements.

(9)   If dogs are fish then they can't swim

38

In any case it seems pointless to say anything about the truth-value of the implication when the antecedent is false. Examples of this type (usually called **counter-factual** sentences) can be made even more manifestly absurd.

(**10**)   If I were invisible everybody would see me

Suppose that (10) is analysed $p \to q$ and that p is false, which is empirically probable. Then $p \to q$ automatically by the truth-conditions of the implication becomes true.

(**11**)   If I were invisible nobody would see me.

(11), which seems much more reasonable, would be true for the same reason. There is no way of accounting for our intuition that while (11) seems quite reasonable (10) seems utterly absurd. Both sentences are analysed $p \to q$ and truth-functionally treated the same way.

(**12**)   If Canute was French he was talented
(**13**)   If Canute was French he was not talented

Even though (13) says the opposite of (12) both must be regarded as true if we analyse antecedent and consequent as united by material implication, since the common antecedent of both is false.

Even if the analysis of *if...then* as material implication is inadequate on most counts, there are a few things that speak in its favour. It seems that the ordinary-language counterparts of logical expressions which are truth-functionally equivalent to $p \to q$ have much the same force as the ordinary-language counterparts of $p \to q$. $\sim p \vee q$ is truth-functionally equivalent to $p \to q$. The truth table of the material implication tells us that it is true if either its antecedent clause is false or its consequent clause true. This is exactly what is expressed by $\sim p \vee q$: 'antecedent false or consequent true'. This can be ascertained by constructing the truth table for $\sim p \vee q$.

(14) and (15) are ordinary-language counterparts of $p \to q$ and $\sim p \vee q$ respectively.

(**14**)   If I am right I owe you $10
(**15**)   Either I am wrong or I owe you $10

As we see, they have much the same meaning. This does lend some indirect support to the truth-functional analysis of *if...then* that we have stipulated. There have also been attempts to use the material implication as the basis for an analysis of *if...then* which utilizes communicative norms of the type we discussed in connection with the disjunction.[4] The somewhat absurd results of analysing *if...then* as → which we discussed above are then explained as violations of such general communicative norms.

The set-theoretical counterpart of the implication is not as straightforward as the ones we have discussed for the other connectives. In (16), A and B are the truth-sets for p and q respectively and the shaded area is the truth-set for $p \to q$. (A good exercise is to check that it corresponds to the truth table on p. 38.)

(**16**)

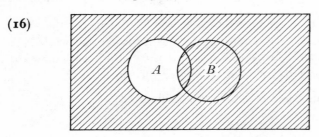

4.2.5. *Equivalence*

Equivalence roughly corresponds to *if and only if, exactly when, only when, only if*. Sometimes even simple *if* is used to indicate equivalence. Truth-functionally an equivalence is analysed as a double material implication, one going from antecedent to consequent and another going from consequent to antecedent. Since the analysis of the equivalence is based on the analysis of the implication, some of the same problems concerning the ordinary-language counterparts of implication turn up in connection with equivalence.

Another problem which sometimes causes difficulty is how to differentiate between equivalence and implication. We will attempt to clarify the distinction with two examples.

(**1**)   Mary will pass the exam if her result on the written test is satisfactory

(**2**)   Mary will pass the exam if and only if her result on the written test is satisfactory

In (1), 'passing the written test' is a **sufficient** but not **necessary** requirement for Mary to pass the exam. Orals, red apples or even a mild

---

[4] For this type of treatment, see Grice (1975).

flirtation could be other sufficient means. In (2), however, passing the written test is not only a sufficient condition but also a necessary condition for passing the exam. Nothing else will do.

Since an equivalence is a conjunction of two implications, we obtain the following truth table for equivalence. As special symbol we use $\equiv$ ($\leftrightarrow$ or $\rightleftharpoons$ is sometimes used). Very often 'if and only if' is abbreviated 'iff'.

(3)

p	q	$p \equiv q$
t	t	t
t	f	f
f	t	f
f	f	t

As we can see, the equivalence is true only when the simple sentences it combines have the same truth-value. If we think of equivalence as a conjunction of two material implications, we understand why this is the case.

(4) $(p \rightarrow q) \,\&\, (q \rightarrow p)$

We know that a conjunction to be true requires that all the sentences that it combines are true. For this condition to be met either p and q both have to be true or both have to be false. If they have different truth-values, the truth-conditions of the material implication will not be met in both sentences simultaneously (the antecedent may not be true and the consequent false), which is required for the conjunction to be true.

The set-theoretical counterpart of equivalence is rather neat and clearly shows that the simultaneity condition on the truth-value of the two sentences is upheld. In (5) the truth-set for $p \equiv q$ is shaded, while A and B represent the truth-sets for p and q respectively.

(5)

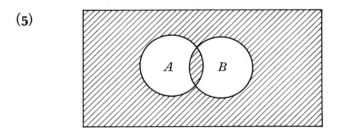

4.3. **How to indicate constituent structure**

In logic as in linguistics, it is of great importance to know how any sequence of symbols is structured, what things go together and what things do not. There are many ways of representing linguistic structure diagrammatically. The most common ways are tree diagrams, box diagrams and parentheses. These are all formally equivalent but differ somewhat in practical application. In logic, parentheses are the most common structure-indicating device.

The most important reason for marking constituent structure in logic is to avoid ambiguity. Without any indication of structure the following expression is hopelessly ambiguous.

(1)   It's snowing and it's raining implies that it will be wet and it will be cold

With sentential variables we write

(2) $p \& q \to r \& s$

We now have the following choices as to what implies what.

(3) $(p \& q) \to (r \& s)$
(4) $p \& (q \to (r \& s))$
(5) $p \& ((q \to r) \& s)$
(6) $((p \& q) \to r) \& s$

The structure possibilities we have indicated by parentheses in (3)–(6) can also be indicated with tree and box diagrams respectively.

TREE DIAGRAMS. We will first give the tree structures without node labels (a node is an intersection of lines in a tree) and then with node labels. The node labels are abbreviated in the following way: Implication = Impl, Conjunction = Conj. The sentential connective which is placed directly under the highest node is called the **main connective** of the sentence. In (3') this is the implication arrow.

(3')

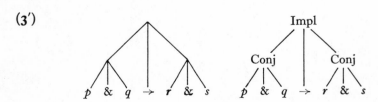

(4′)

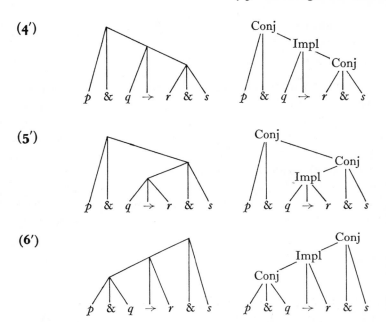

(5′)

(6′)

BOX DIAGRAMS. This time we introduce the labels into the diagram at once.

(3″)

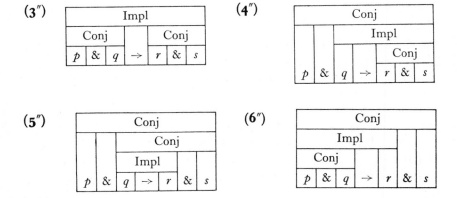

(4″)

(5″)

(6″)

Node labels can of course also be used with parentheses (we then get so-called labelled parentheses). Implication is abbreviated I and conjunction C.

(3‴) $(_I(_Cp \ \& \ q) \to (_Cr \ \& \ s)_C)_I$

(4‴) $\qquad (_\mathrm{C}p \ \& \ (_\mathrm{I}q \rightarrow (_\mathrm{C}r \ \& \ s)_\mathrm{C})_\mathrm{I})_\mathrm{C}$

(5‴) $\qquad (_\mathrm{C}p \ \& \ (_\mathrm{C}(_\mathrm{I}q \rightarrow r)_\mathrm{I} \ \& \ s)_\mathrm{C})_\mathrm{C}$

(6‴) $\qquad (_\mathrm{C}(_\mathrm{I}(_\mathrm{C}p \ \& \ q)_\mathrm{C} \rightarrow r)_\mathrm{I} \ \& \ s)_\mathrm{C}$

Before we leave this digression, it should be said that normally parentheses are used in logic only to the extent that they are necessary for the sake of clarity. Very often the following conventions are followed: if no parentheses follow a negation sign, the **scope** of the negation is always taken to be the smallest possible, i.e. it applies to the closest minimal constituent to its right. In general, the scope of a logical operator is the parts of an expression that are affected by the operator. This can be indicated by direct contiguity as for negation or by parentheses, where everything enclosed between two matching parentheses will make up the scope.

(7) $\qquad \sim p \ \& \ q$

(8) $\qquad \sim (p \ \& \ q) \ \& \ r$

Thus in (7) the negation applies only to p and not to the whole conjunction, while in (8) the inserted parentheses force it to apply to the left-most conjunction, but again not to the expression as a whole. Similarly & and $\vee$ are often given shorter scope than $\rightarrow$ and $\equiv$. If we accept these conventions, our example (2)

(2) $\qquad p \ \& \ q \rightarrow r \ \& \ s$

becomes unambiguous and should be interpreted as $(p \ \& \ q) \rightarrow (r \ \& \ s)$. However, we shall not be following these conventions except with negation, and will use parentheses when we think they are called for to avoid ambiguity.

4.4. The syntax and semantics of propositional calculus

We have now come far enough to be able to give a summary of the smallest simple symbols of propositional logic. We can also give a set of rules that tells us how these symbols may be combined into bigger units. The rules have the property of expressing exactly what combinations are allowed and what combinations are excluded.

The enumeration of the smallest simple symbols is usually referred to in logic as the **vocabulary**. It has the same function that a dictionary has for a natural language. The rules that state the allowable combinations of simple units – so-called **well-formed formulas (wff)** – are often called the **rules of formation** and can be compared to the grammatical rules of a natural language. The vocabulary and the rules of formation together make up the **syntax** of the logic. The syntax tells us nothing about how they are to be interpreted, i.e. what their meaning is. This is studied in the **semantics**.

We are now in a position to attempt a definition of what a formal language is. A formal language is a set of expressions which is such that it is correlated to a vocabulary from which the expressions are constructed according to the rules of syntax and interpreted by the rules of semantics. An important distinction to be made here is the distinction between speaking IN such a language and speaking ABOUT such a language. The language itself – the object we are investigating – is called the **object language**, and the language we are using to investigate the object language in is called the **metalanguage**. The language we use in grammar or in logic when we talk about other languages can thus be characterized as metalanguage.

4.5. **Syntax**

To give the syntax of propositional logic we start by giving its vocabulary.

(1) VOCABULARY

(i) Infinitely many sentential variables: $p, q, r, s, t, p_1, q_1, \ldots p_2$
$q_2 \ldots$
(ii) The logical connectives: $\sim$, &, $\vee$, $\rightarrow$, $\equiv$
(iii) Parentheses: ( )
(iv) These and no other signs occur in the expressions of propositional logic

Secondly we must indicate what combinations of signs are allowed – the well-formed formulas. We will therefore give the rules of formation for propositional logic.

(2) RULES OF FORMATION

(i) Every sentential variable is a wff
(ii) If α and β are arbitrary wffs, then (a) $\sim \alpha$, (b) $(\alpha \& \beta)$, (c) $(\alpha \vee \beta)$, (d) $(\alpha \rightarrow \beta)$ and (e) $(\alpha \equiv \beta)$ are also wffs
(iii) An expression is only a wff if it has been constructed by these rules

45

In rule (ii) we want to make it clear that we are talking about a language in a metalanguage and have therefore introduced so-called **meta-variables** (the Greek letters α, β) instead of the sentential variables one might have expected. We have done this to indicate that we are here speaking not about arbitrary SIMPLE sentences but about any arbitrarily chosen wff of propositional logic. Everything that is a wff can thus be substituted for α or β. These rules can therefore be applied to their own results. Take for example the two wffs p and q. From these in accordance with rule (ii)(b) we construct $p \,\&\, q$. However, we can apply rule (ii)(b) once more and get $(p \,\&\, q) \,\&\, p$. α is substituted for $p \,\&\, q$, which is a wff. In this way, we can, through a step-by-step application of the rules, generate as long and as complex expressions as we want. Rules that have this property are called **recursive** and have played a large role in the development of generative grammar and many computer languages. The procedure of applying recursive rules is often referred to as (mathematical) **induction.**

Syntactic rules being recursive, we can construct an indefinitely large set of expressions with a finite set of rules. Since any natural language contains an indefinitely large number of grammatical sentences, the grammar of natural language must probably contain recursive rules.

The following expressions are examples of wffs. Here we shall not use the external parentheses of rule (ii), which were introduced only to exclude ambiguity: p, q, $p \,\&\, q$, $(p \,\&\, q) \to q$, $p \lor q$, $(p \,\&\, q) \equiv (p \lor q)$. The following expressions are not wffs: $\&\, q$, $\lor\, r \to p$, $q \sim\, \to p$.

Rules (2)(i) and (2)(ii) can also be written in the following equivalent way.

(3)(i)

$$S \to \begin{cases} \sim S \\ (S \,\&\, S) \\ (S \lor S) \\ (S \to S) \\ (S \equiv S) \end{cases}$$

(ii) $\quad S \to p, q \ldots p_1, q_1 \ldots p_2, q_2 \ldots$

If they are written this way they have been given the same format as what are usually called **phrase-structure rules** in generative grammar. As rule (2)(iii) in such a grammar is always understood to hold by implicit convention, rules (3)(i) and (ii) therefore provide an alternative and equivalent description of the syntax of propositional logic.

4.6. **Semantics**

In describing the syntax of propositional logic we regard all the symbols of the logic as 'empty', without meaning. But we are, of course, also interested in using logic for inferences about the world around us. As soon as we relate the signs we are studying to other phenomena for which they are signs, we have taken the step from syntax to **semantics**. Semantics is the study of how those expressions which are allowed by the syntax are related to what the expressions are about.

Since in logic we are primarily interested in sentences, it is the meaning of sentences we want to study. One of the best ways to understand the meaning of a sentence is to imagine what the world would have to be like for the sentence to be true.

(**1**)   Baron Münchhausen pulled himself out of the water by lifting himself by the hair

The reason why (1) is difficult to understand is that it is hard to imagine what the world would have to be like for (1) to be true. The concept of truth thus gives us a fine instrument for getting at the relation between sentences and what they are about. We can characterize an important part of the meaning of a sentence by formulating the conditions the world must meet for the sentence to be true (in other words, we say in what worlds the sentence is true). These conditions are called the **truth-conditions** of the sentence. In logic the meaning of a sentence is equated with its truth-conditions. This, of course, means that some important aspects of meaning are disregarded, but an analysis of this type is still very satisfactory for the purposes of logic, as we are interested only in those aspects of meaning that have a role to play in logical truth and logical inference. (We shall return to this question in chapter 10.)

As propositional logic treats simple sentences as unanalysed wholes, we cannot within the limits of propositional logic say anything about the truth-conditions of individual simple sentences. We can, however, say a fair amount about how the truth-conditions of compound sentences are related to the simple sentences from which they are constructed.

More precisely, in propositional logic we are interested in how the truth-values of compound sentences are determined by the truth-values of their constituent sentences and the choice of logical connectives. Thus the only relevant property, here, of a simple sentence is its truth-value. In order to study what happens in compound sentences a truth-value is usually arbitrarily assigned to each simple sentential variable. (It would of course be possible to use real sentences and check the truth-value of each sentence, but this has limited interest as long as we are interested in the effect of the connective on the truth-value of the compound sentence, given any set of truth-values of its constituent sentences.)

Using the information we have given in the truth table for each logical connective above, we will now give the truth-conditions for compound sentences. We will again use Greek letters as metavariables for arbitrary expressions, which means that our truth-conditions will be recursive. They can be applied again and again to give the truth-conditions of increasingly complex expressions. We are also once more differentiating between the language of investigation – the metalanguage – and the language we are investigating – the object language. We are giving the truth-conditions for the object language and are thus not attempting any analysis of the metalanguage, which we are simply taking as understood. The symbol 'iff' which we use below is part of the metalanguage – part of our description of the truth-conditions of the object language – and should therefore be separated from $\equiv$, which is a symbol of the object language, the language we are investigating. (2) below gives the truth-conditions recursively for the compound sentences of propositional logic.

(2)   THE SEMANTICS OF PROPOSITIONAL LOGIC

  (i) $\sim \alpha$ is true iff α is not true
  (ii) $\alpha \,\&\, \beta$ is true iff both α and β are true
  (iii) $\alpha \lor \beta$ is true iff at least one of the expressions α and β is true
  (iv) $\alpha \to \beta$ is true iff α is not true or β true
  (v) $\alpha \equiv \beta$ is true iff α and β have the same truth-value

Using these truth-conditions we can compute the truth-value of an expression of arbitrary complexity. Let us consider some examples.

(3) $(p \,\&\, (q \lor p)) \to (p \lor r) \,\&\, q)$

We now assume that truth-values have been assigned to the variables; this can be done by arbitrary assignment or by substituting a declarative sentence for each variable and then assigning its truth-value. We are assuming that this has been done and that the variables were assigned the following truth-values: p is true; q and r are false.

Let us represent the example diagrammatically as an upside-down tree structure in order to see how the truth-values of the simple expressions determine those of the complex ones. Disjunction, negation and equivalence are abbreviated as 'Disj', 'Neg' and 'Eq' respectively; conjunction and implication, as before, by 'Conj' and 'Impl'.

(4)

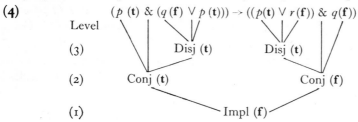

The disjunctions on level (3) are both true, as at least one of the simple sentences in each is true. On level (2) only the first conjunction is true, as both its subordinate sentences (one of them being itself compound) are true. The other conjunction is false, as one of its subordinate conjuncts is false.

The implication on level (1) is false, since its antecedent is true but its consequent false. The truth-value of the complex expression is therefore **f**. It is worth noticing that in computing the value of the complex expression, we have, in a manner of speaking, been working from the inside to the outside. We start with the constituents which are most deeply embedded and smallest in size and end up with the biggest. Innermost parentheses first! Those who are familiar with transformational grammar in Chomsky's (1965) version may observe that this principle also holds for the cyclical rules of syntax and phonology and the projection rules of semantics. The final example is an equivalence which we leave to the reader.

(5)

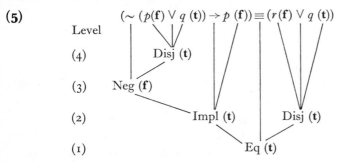

p and *r* have been assigned **f**, while *q* has received **t**.

4.7. **Tautologies and contradictions**

There are certain complex expressions that always receive 'true' as their computed truth-value irrespective of the assignment of truth-values to the simple sentences of the expression. These are of special interest in logic, as the truth-value of such expressions can be said to be completely determined by the truth-functional properties of the logical connectives – by the logical forms of the expressions. Such complex sentences are called **tautologies**. There are also sentences that always receive **f** as the value of the whole expression, irrespective of the truth-value of the simple sentences. These are called **contradictions**.

Since a tautology is always true, it is a logical truth, but there are logical truths that are not tautologies, as we shall see below. In the same way that logical truth is a wider concept than tautology, analytic truth is a wider concept than logical truth (see p. 23 above).

A simple example of a tautology can be obtained by disjunctively combining a sentence with its own negation.

(1) $p \vee \sim p$ (It's raining or it's not raining)

Whatever sentence we use for p and whatever truth-value we give this sentence, the truth-value of the complex expression will be **t** – a logical truth. Another way of putting this is to say, 'However we change the world (whatever world we choose), it will be true that *either the moon is a piece of green cheese or it is not.*' In other words, the truth-set of a tautology is always the set of all possible worlds (the universal set). I.e. it is easy to see that the set of possible worlds where $p \vee \sim p$ is true is the union of the set of possible worlds where p is true and the set of possible worlds where $\sim p$ is true, which is the same as the set of all possible worlds (the universal set). More generally, it holds that the truth-set of a tautology is the universal set and that the truth-set of a contradiction is the empty set.

4.8. **Truth tables**

It would be nice to have a mechanical means of deciding whether a sentence is a tautology or not. Such a means exists in propositional logic. It is the so-called **truth-table method**.

We partly used this method when we studied the truth-functional properties of the connectives. We will now see how this method can be applied to compound sentences with several different connectives.

The purpose of the method is to check whether a sentence is a tautology, a contradiction or neither. What we will do, therefore, is simply to investigate every possible combination of truth-values for the simple sentences and then check the resulting truth-value of the complex expression. For $p \lor \sim p$ there are two possibilities: either p is true or p is false. If p is true, its negation is false and vice versa.

A disjunction of p and its negation must therefore always be true, since in each case one of the disjuncts is true. In the truth-table format we write:

(1)
p	$\sim p$	$p \lor \sim p$
t	f	t
f	t	t

(1) can also be written as (1′).

(1′)
p	$\sim p$
t	t f t
f	t t f

If we have two sentential variables we have four possibilities; if we have three there are eight possibilities (more generally there are always 2^n possibilities, where n is the number of different sentential variables and 2, the base, is the number of truth-values).

Let us study two more examples.

(2) $(p \,\&\, q) \to p$

p	q	$p \,\&\, q$	p	$(p \,\&\, q) \to p$
t	t	t	t	t
t	f	f	t	t
f	t	f	f	t
f	f	f	f	t

Whatever truth-values we assign to the simple sentences we get a true sentence. Thus (2) is a tautology.

(3) $(p \,\&\, q) \to (p \lor r)$

p	q	r	$p \,\&\, q$	$p \lor r$	$(p \,\&\, q) \to (p \lor r)$
t	t	t	t	t	t
t	t	f	t	t	t
t	f	t	f	t	t
t	f	f	f	t	t

p	q	r	$p\,\&\,q$	$p \vee r$	$(p\,\&\,q) \rightarrow (p \vee r)$
f	t	t	f	t	t
f	t	f	f	f	t
f	f	t	f	t	t
f	f	f	f	f	t

Again a tautology, since the result of all the possible combinations of truth-values of the constituents is **t**.

But all sentences in propositional logic are no tautologies:

(4) $\sim p \rightarrow (p \vee q)$

p	q	$\sim p$	$p \vee q$	$\sim p \rightarrow p \vee q$
t	t	f	t	t
t	f	f	t	t
f	t	t	t	t
f	f	t	f	f

(4) is neither a contradiction nor a tautology but is what we have above called a synthetic sentence: a sentence the truth-value of which is dependent on what the world is like. The characteristic property of a synthetic sentence is the mixture of **t**'s and **f**'s in the final row under the main connective of the expression. This means that the truth-value of the complex sentence depends on the truth-values of the constituent sentences; and the truth-values of the simple sentences are, of course, dependent on what the world is like. This is why we say that compound sentences that are neither tautologies nor contradictions are synthetic sentences, i.e. sentences whose truth-values are a matter of what the world is like.

(5) $\sim (p \rightarrow (p \vee q))$

p	q	$p \vee q$	$p \rightarrow (p \vee q)$	$\sim (p \rightarrow (p \vee q))$
t	t	t	t	f
t	f	t	t	f
f	t	t	t	f
f	f	f	t	f

(5) is a contradiction. All possible combinations of truth-values yield the final value **f**.

Contradictions of the type exemplified by (5) illustrate the relationship between contradiction and tautology. $p \rightarrow (p \vee q)$ is, as we can see, a tautology, while $\sim (p \rightarrow (p \vee q))$ is a contradiction. By negating a tautology we get a contradiction just as by negating a contradiction we get a tautology.

One can compare the logical form of a sentence, which in propositional logic is determined by the truth-functional properties of the connectives, to a machine, into which one inserts the truth-values of simple sentences and out of which one receives truth-values of compound sentences. If one receives **t** irrespective of what truth-value one has inserted, one is dealing with a tautology.

This machine-like quality of logical form is dependent on the fact that each logical connective relates each possible combination of truth-values in a specific way to the truth-value of the compound sentence. The structural relations between sentences which are studied in propositional logic can thus be said to be those relations that hold between sentences with respect to their truth-values. What a logical connective does is to decide, for each possible combination of truth-values, what the resulting truth-value is for that combination. The truth-value of a compound sentence is unambiguously determined by the logical connective and the possible truth-value combinations of the simple sentences.

It is therefore natural to say that the connectives designate functions that map one or several truth-values onto one and only one truth-value. We call such functions **truth-functions**.

We have everywhere, except in example (3), chosen our examples of how to compute truth-values so that we had to handle only two variables. The reason for this is that the number of possible truth-value combinations rises exponentially with the number of different sentential variables; the computations will therefore, if nothing else, be very boring to perform. In expressions with more than two variables we therefore try to use so-called **indirect reasoning** (often also called **reductio ad absurdum**).

In reasoning indirectly we proceed in the following way. We assume that the expression we are interested in is false. If this assumption does not lead to a contradiction, we know that we do not have a tautology. This must be so since a tautology is characterized by always being true. If it is at all possible for the expression we are interested in to be false, the expression cannot be a tautology. However, if our first assumption that the expression is false leads to a contradiction (i.e. it is not possible for the expression to be false), we have a tautology.

If we have shown that assuming a certain sentence to be false does not lead to a contradiction, it still remains to determine whether the sentence is a contradiction or a synthetic sentence. This problem is mostly left unresolved since, in logic, we are primarily interested in determining whether an expression is a tautology or not. If we are interested in the problem of determining whether a sentence is a contradiction, we simply reverse the process of reasoning by assuming that the compound sentence is true and checking whether this leads to a contradiction.

Let us consider some examples of indirect reasoning.

(6)   Level $((p \lor q) \mathbin{\&} r) \to p$

Level				
(1)			**f**	
(2)		**t**	**f**	
(3)	**t**	**t**		
(4)	**f**	**t**		

On level (1) we assume the main truth-value of the implication to be **f**. Our knowledge of the truth-table of material implication tells us that an implication can only be false if its antecedent is true and its consequent false, which is what we have indicated on level (2). The two **t**'s on level (3) are a result of the truth-conditions for the conjunction which has been made **t** on level (2). A conjunction is true only if both its conjuncts are true. Level (4) is determined by the fact that we have already assigned **f** to p on level (2) – a variable must have the same value everywhere in the same truth-value assignment. We also make use of the fact that the disjunction on level (3) has been assigned the value **t**. According to the truth-conditions of the disjunction, q must now be assigned **t**. As we did not arrive at a contradiction by assuming that (6) was false, (6) cannot be a tautology.

(7)   Level $(((\sim p \to \sim (q \lor r)) \mathbin{\&} (s \to r)) \mathbin{\&} s) \to p$

Level								
							f	
(2)						**t**	**f**	
(3)				**t**		**t**		
(4)		**t**			**t**			
(5)	**t**	**f**^{1}	**t**	**f**	**t**^{2}	**t***		
(6)			**f**	**f***			contradiction	

The two values assigned to p and s on level (5) (marked by superscript (1) and (2) respectively) are directly transferred from the assignments made on levels (2) and (3) respectively.

In this example we will let the reader himself do the reasoning, drawing on his knowledge of the truth-functional properties of the connectives.

We will just say in conclusion that (7), as should be clear, leads to a contradiction (see the two variables marked by *). We are forced to assume both that r is false and that r is true. As this is a contradiction, we are led to the conclusion that (7) cannot be false. It must therefore be a tautology.

How do we handle sentences the main connectives of which are not implications? For example, if we assume a conjunction to be false there are three possibilities to investigate. The heroic way is to investigate each possibility by the methods we have indicated above. There is, however, another possibility. We can use our knowledge of logical equivalence to rewrite expressions which are not implications as implications. We list below some well-known logically true sentences and equivalences, some of which can be used to rewrite a logical expression as an implication, thus making a reductio inference easier.

(8)　(i)　$p \lor \sim p$
　　(ii)　$\sim (p \,\&\, \sim p)$
　　(iii)　$p \equiv p$
　　(iv)　$(p \lor q) \equiv \sim (\sim p \,\&\, \sim q)$
　　(v)　$(p \,\&\, q) \equiv \sim (\sim p \lor \sim q)$
　　(vi)　$\sim (p \lor q) \equiv (\sim p \,\&\, \sim q)$
　　(vii)　$\sim (p \,\&\, q) \equiv (\sim p \lor \sim q)$
　　(viii)　$(p \to q) \equiv \sim (p \,\&\, \sim q)$
　　(ix)　$(p \,\&\, q) \equiv \sim (p \to \sim q)$
　　(x)　$\sim (p \to q) \equiv (p \,\&\, \sim q)$
　　(xi)　$\sim (p \,\&\, q) \equiv (p \to \sim q)$
　　(xii)　$(p \lor q) \equiv (\sim p \to q)$
　　(xiii)　$(p \to q) \equiv (\sim p \lor q)$
　　(xiv)　$\sim \sim p \equiv p$
　　(xv)　$p \equiv p \lor p$

Using any of these tautologies and equivalences or other similar ones[5] the reader can easily transform an expression into a form which is easy to handle. Consider (9).

(9)　　　$\sim (((p \,\&\, (q \lor \sim q)) \to p) \,\&\, \sim p)$

(9) looks formidable so we change it into (10) using (8) (xi).

(10)　　　$((p \,\&\, (q \lor \sim q)) \to p) \to \sim \sim p$

---

[5] For a much more extensive treatment of tautologies in propositional logic, see Kalish and Montague (1964) or Thomason (1970).

At least we now have an implication that we can try indirect reasoning on. If we change (10) into (11):

(11) $((p \,\&\, (q \lor \sim q)) \to p) \to p$
          f f   t t f   t   t   t f f f

and try a reductio argument, we find that (9) is not a tautology.

EXERCISES

1. Which of the following three sentences cannot be formalized like the others in propositional logic and why?

   (a) Oliver and Richard are Roundheads
   (b) Oliver and Richard are relatives
   (c) Oliver and Richard like to drink

2. Try to represent the following sentences with sentential variables and logical connectives.

   (a) If this is summer it's damned cold
   (b) Lemons look good but taste sour
   (c) You can if you want to
   (d) He will come today or tomorrow but not later
   (e) If neither God nor the Devil exists it's difficult to be religious
   (f) Throw the cat out or I will leave

3. Give the truth-values of the following compound expressions where we assume that p and q are true and r is false.

   (a) $\sim p$
   (b) $\sim (p \,\&\, r)$
   (c) $\sim (p \lor q)$
   (d) $p \lor (q \,\&\, r)$
   (e) $r \to ((q \,\&\, r) \lor (p \lor q))$
   (f) $r \equiv (p \,\&\, r)$

4. Which of the following expressions are tautologies?

   (a) $\sim (p \,\&\, \sim p)$
   (b) $(p \lor q) \to p$
   (c) $\sim (p \,\&\, q) \equiv \sim p \lor \sim q$
   (d) $\sim ((p \equiv q) \equiv (p \equiv \sim q))$
   (e) $(p \to \sim q) \lor (q \to \sim p)$
   (f) $((p \equiv q) \equiv p) \equiv q$
   (g) $(p \,\&\, q) \lor (p \equiv \sim q)$
   (h) $(p \lor (q \,\&\, r)) \equiv ((p \lor q) \,\&\, (p \lor r))$

5. Is the conjunction *because* a truth-functional connective? Give reasons for your answer.

6. The term **Polish bracket-free notation** means that a connective is written on the left of the sentences it combines instead of as usual in between them. The connectives are in this case usually abbreviated as follows: N = negation, A = disjunction ('alternation'), K = conjunction, C = implication ('conditional'), E = equivalence.
   Examples:

Standard notation	Polish notation
$\sim p$	Np
$p \ \& \ q$	Kpq
$p \rightarrow q$	Cpq
$(p \rightarrow q) \ \& \ p$	KCpqp
$(p \ \& \ q) \vee (p \ \& \ r)$	AKpqKpr

   Now write the following expressions in Polish notation.

   (*a*) $p \vee q$
   (*b*) $\sim p \equiv q$
   (*c*) $(p \vee q) \equiv (p \ \& \ q)$

7. Write the following Polish expressions in standard notation.

   (*a*) KpNq
   (*b*) CAKE$pqrst$
   (*c*) ECpqCNqNp

8. Determine by indirect reasoning whether the following expressions are tautologies.

   (*a*) $p \rightarrow (q \rightarrow (r \rightarrow (s \rightarrow (t \rightarrow p))))$
   (*b*) $((p \equiv q) \ \& \ (q \equiv r)) \rightarrow (p \equiv r)$
   (*c*) $(p \ \& \ (q \equiv r)) \rightarrow ((p \ \& \ q) \equiv r)$

5
Predicate logic

5.1. **Extending the logical analysis**

In the chapter about propositional logic, it was shown that we could decide whether inferences and sentences were correct or true (tautological) by using such techniques as the truth-table method.

However, we can express many inferences in natural language which are intuitively felt to be correct but which cannot be shown to be correct in propositional logic, e.g. (1).

(1)   If all moose are clever and Bruce is a moose, then Bruce is clever

The reasoning in these sentences seems sound to everyone, yet it cannot be shown to be correct in propositional logic. (1) would be analysed as $(p \ \& \ q) \rightarrow r$ in propositional logic, which can be shown to be anything but tautological by a truth table. Predicate logic, on the other hand, gives us an instrument with which we can show that the inference in (1) is correct. In general, it can be said that predicate logic takes us from those logical relations that hold between sentences to those that hold within a sentence.

We will now examine in more detail how this is done. Let us start with a simple sentence.

(2)   Bruce is a moose

This sentence says something about an individual. The individual is Bruce and it is said of him that he has the property of being a moose. Such sentences are called **predications** – one predicates something (e.g. a property) of an individual.

The linguistic parallel subject-phrase and predicate-phrase can be helpful to some extent in developing the relevant intuition here.

The following sentences all have the same logical form as (2) in that they predicate something of an individual.

(3)　　　The bear is asleep
　　　　King Canute surrendered
　　　　Olaf was a Viking
　　　　The east is red

The subjects in the sentences above are written *a, b, c, d, ...* These symbols are called **individual constants** (lower-case italic letters). The predicates in the sentences above are written *A, B, C, D, ...* These symbols are called **predicate constants** or simply **predicates** (italic capital letters).

Now we can formalize sentence (2) in predicate logic. For simplicity's sake, we assign the letter *b* to Bruce and the letter *M* to the property of being a moose. The sentence is represented as follows. By convention, the predicate is placed first in the expression.

(4)　　　$M(b)$

In (4), we speak about a certain individual, Bruce, and a certain property being a moose, and say that Bruce has the property of being a moose. We can also form the following expression.

(5)　　　$M(x)$

In this expression, *x* is not an individual constant but an **individual variable**. This means that *x* does not stand for a particular individual but for any individual (or, in other words, *x* stands for an arbitrary individual). As it stands, (5) does not express any proposition. Therefore, (5) is not called a sentence in predicate logic but rather an **open sentence** (see p. 63 for further discussion of open sentences).

We can go one step further on the abstraction scale and form the following expression.

(6)　　　$\Phi(x)$

In this formula, we have not only an individual variable but also a **predicate variable**, Φ (the capital Greek letter phi). A predicate variable does not stand for a particular property but for any property (an arbitrary property). As it stands, (6) is a rather meaningless expression. It indicates the possibility of predicating an arbitrary property of an arbitrary individual. (6) makes no existential claim. However, as will be shown below, expressions like (6) can be used for certain purposes in logic.

Individual constants and individual variables are grouped together under the name **individual terms**. In the same way, predicate constants and predicate variables are grouped together under the term **predicate terms**.

The sentences given in (2) and (3) can all be said to have the same structure or the same logical form. They consist of a predicate term (P) followed by an individual term (t). Hence, they all have the logical form represented in (7).

(7) $P(t)$

Obviously, not all sentences have the logical form of (7). The following sentences have another logical form.

(8)   Thor stole the hammer
         Wotan admires Thor
         God created the world
         Wotan is wiser than Thor

In these sentences, we find predicates that take two arguments. **Argument** is a term that is used to refer to, among other things, what are called subjects and objects in grammatical terminology. The individual terms that follow the predicate in an expression in predicate logic are called the arguments of that predicate. If a predicate takes one argument, it is called a one-place predicate; if it takes two arguments it is called a two-place predicate, and so on. This terminology is illustrated in (9).

(9) $P(t)$ one-place predicate
         $P(t_1, t_2)$ two-place predicate
         $P(t_1, t_2, t_3)$ three-place predicate
         $P(t_1, t_2, t_3, t_4)$ four-place predicate
         $P(t_1, t_2 \ldots t_n)$ n-place predicate

Since the predicates in (8), *stole, admires, created* and *is wiser than*, each take two arguments, they are two-place predicates. The sentences in (8), consequently, have the logical form $P(t_1, t_2)$. The sentences in (10) can be formalized as $P(t_1, t_2, t_3)$, i.e. they contain three-place predicates. The arguments are underlined.

(10)   Jack gave Jill the apple
             The guide showed the tourist Gothenburg
             Wotan offered Thor beer

It is hard to find sentences in natural language that illustrate predicates that take more than three arguments without going into controversial matters. The following sentence, however, might be said to illustrate the use of a four-place predicate.

(11)   Jack bought Jill a watch for five pounds

In the sentences above, we have given some examples where the predicates in the logical formulas correspond fairly well to the predicates of the grammatical analysis. For a logician, it is, however, a matter of little interest whether a logical predicate corresponds to a certain word or a certain simple expression in natural language. In logic, very complex expressions like *eats porridge between 10 and 11 on Sunday mornings* or *is a long-haired linguist who is interested in the relation between modal logic and dialectology* can be regarded as predicates in a logical formula. This means that a sentence like *Thor stole the hammer* does not have to be analysed as $F(a, b)$, with a two-place predicate, even though this would be the most natural way of analysing the sentence from a linguistic point of view, but that this sentence in principle could also be analysed as $F(a)$, with a one-place predicate, where F would stand for the predicate *stole the hammer*.

5.2. Quantifiers

Let us now return to the first clause of the first example in this chapter.

(1)   All moose are clever

If we were to analyse this sentence as we analysed other sentences in this chapter, we would get

(2) $C(\text{all moose})$

in the same way as

(3) $C(\text{Bruce})$

The problem with (2) is that we cannot substitute an individual constant for the expression *all moose*. This expression does not refer to an individual as the name *Bruce* does. What (2) really says is that if we find a moose, we can expect it to be clever. This can be expressed in another way: pick an arbitrary moose and you will find him to be clever.

In order to analyse sentences like (1), we introduce a new type of logical constant: **the universal quantifier**, with the meaning 'all', 'every' or 'for everyone/everything holds that'. The universal quantifier is represented by the symbol ∀. A sentence like Heraclitus' *Everything is in a state of flux* is formalized in the following way by using the universal quantifier.

(4) $\forall x \, F(x)$

This can be read 'For every x, it holds that x is in flux'. In a similar manner, (1) can be analysed as (5).

(5) $\forall x \, (M(x) \to C(x))$

This expression can be read in any of the following ways.

(6)   (a) For every x, it holds that if x is a moose then x is clever
       (b) For everything, it holds that if it is a moose then it is clever
       (c) If something is a moose then it is clever
       (d) All moose are clever

In order to understand how formulas like (5) function, it is important to know what a variable is. The x in $\forall x$ stands for any individual in the universe. It ranges over all individuals and objects in the universe: its **range** is all individuals and objects in the universe.

The range need not be everything in the universe we live in, although that is the case in the example above. In a mathematical text, the range could be the set of all numbers, and in a sociological text, the set of all human beings, and so on. The concept **universe of discourse** is used in this context, i.e. everything that we speak about in a certain context. This concept was introduced in chapter 2.

To achieve a better understanding of the difference between simple sentences like $F(b)$ ('Bruce is in a state of flux') and quantified sentences like $\forall x \, F(x)$ ('Everything is in a state of flux'), we return to the concept of open sentences. An open sentence is an expression of the form (7).

(7) $F(x)$ (reads 'x is in a state of flux')

Since x is a variable that does not refer to any individual in particular, we cannot meaningfully say that $F(x)$ expresses a proposition or makes a statement. It cannot be said that an open sentence is true or false. A simple sentence like *Bruce is in a state of flux*, on the other hand, is always true or false – it has a truth-value. How can the question 'Is it true that x is in a state of flux?' be answered? The only thing we can answer is 'It depends on who or what x is.' If x refers to the Thames, it is true, but if x refers to King Canute, it might not be. To say that King Canute does not satisfy the open sentence $F(x)$ is equivalent to saying that $F(c)$, where c refers to King Canute, is a false sentence.

One way to make a sentence out of an open sentence is to assign a certain value to the variable. As we have indicated above, this is effected by substituting an individual constant for the variable in the formula. Open sentences are also called **sentential functions**. We can understand this term by regarding the open sentence as a function that takes different individuals as arguments and that gives different sentences as values. Another way to make a sentence of an open sentence is to place a quantifier followed by a variable in front of the open sentence. This brings us back to the sentence we had above.

(8) $\forall x \, F(x)$ 'Everything is in a state of flux'

(8) says that all objects in the universe of discourse satisfy the open sentence $F(x)$. This is obvious. If there had been one object, say a, in the universe of discourse that did not satisfy the open sentence, then the statement 'Everything is in a state of flux' would have been false. Hence, if $F(a)$ is a false sentence, it makes the quantified sentence $\forall x \, F(x)$ false, given that a is included in the range of x (i.e. that a belongs to the universe of discourse).

It is important to note that we quantify open sentences and not sentences. To quantify an ordinary sentence gives a strange result.

(9) $\forall x \, F(b)$

(9) reads something like 'For every x, it holds that Bruce is in a state of flux', which is nonsense.

Nevertheless, this type of quantification, which is called **vacuous quantification**, since it has no bearing on the meaning of the sentence, is permitted according to most textbooks of logic, the reason being that it simplifies the syntactic rules. (9) is then interpreted as being equivalent to the simple sentence $F(b)$. From a linguistic point of view, vacuous quantification has little or no intuitive content, and in the syntactic rules formulated below, we do not allow it.

Not only simple predications can be described by open sentences but also more complex structures like (10), for example.

(10) $M(x) \rightarrow C(x)$ 'If x is a moose then x is clever'

If we take (10) and put parentheses around it and a quantifier in front of it, we get a sentence.

(11) $\forall x\, (M(x) \rightarrow C(x))$

It is important to note that even though we may pick any individual for x, it is always one and the same individual we have in mind in the two expressions $M(x)$ and $C(x)$ when they are included in the same parentheses, as in (11). We say that the quantifier $\forall x$ **binds** the x's in $M(x)$ and $C(x)$.

The **scope** of a quantifier is the length of the parenthesis that comes immediately after the quantifier (cf. the paragraph on scope in propositional logic on p. 44).

A variable that is bound by a quantifier is called a **bound variable**. Variables that are not bound are called **free variables**, as the last occurrence in (12), for example.

(12) $\forall x\, (F(x) \rightarrow L(x))\ \&\ K(x)$

In (13), however, the corresponding variable is bound.

(13) $\forall x\, (F(x) \rightarrow (L(x)\ \&\ K(x)))$

This means that the value of x in $K(x)$ in the first expression, (12), is independent of the value of the x's that are inside the parentheses. This does not hold for the second expression. In (12), $K(y)$ can be substituted for $K(x)$ without changing the meaning of the expression. This substitution is not possible in (13). Logical formulas that contain free variables do not constitute sentences, but open sentences.

Within the scope of a quantifier, one and the same variable always stands for one and the same individual.

In (14), a number of logical formulas are given where the scope of each quantifier is underlined. We are not interested in what these expressions may mean and what the predicate may stand for. The purpose of these formulas is to make the reader more familiar with the concepts 'scope', 'bound variable', 'free variable' and 'open sentence'.

(**14**) (a) $F(a) \lor \forall x\, (K(x) \to G(x, a))\ \&\ \forall x\, (G(x, a))$

  (b) $\forall x\, (K(x) \to F(y)\ \&\ G(x, a)))$

  (c) $\forall y\, \forall x\, (K(x) \to (F(y)\ \&\ G(x, a)))$

  (d) $\forall x\, ((K(x)\ \&\ F(a)) \to \forall y\, (G(x, y) \lor G(y, y)\ \&\ \forall z$
    $(F(z) \to G(z, y)))$

(14)(a) is not an open sentence, since there are no free variables in it. (14)(b) is an open sentence, since it contains a free variable – the y in $F(y)$. (14)(c) is a sentence with two quantifiers, whose scope overlaps. (14)(d) shows an expression with three quantifiers. The scope of two of these is within the scope of the first one. (14)(d) is not a sentence but an open sentence, because the very last variable of the expression is not bound by any of the quantifiers.

In English, an innumerable set of sentences can be formed that do not contain the quantifier *every* (*all, each*) but some other quantifying word like *one, two, three, some, any, several, many* and *few*. All members of the grammatical category of indefinite pronouns can be regarded as quantifiers of some sort.

In logic, we are usually satisfied with recognizing only two quantifiers. These two quantifiers have the following two characteristics. They are important for the formalization of mathematics and their logical properties are relatively uncomplicated. The first of these two quantifiers is the universal quantifier, which we have discussed above.

The second one is called **the existential quantifier.** It is written $\exists$ and it means something like 'someone/something' or 'there is someone/something'. The following examples show how this quantifier is used.

(**15**) (a) Someone is conservative $\exists x\, C(x)$

  (b) There exists a unicorn $\exists x\, U(x)$

  (c) Some girl is nicer than Jane $\exists x\, (G(x)\ \&\ N(x, j))$

   where C stands for 'conservative'
        U 'being a unicorn'
        G 'being a girl'
        N 'being nicer than'
        j Jane

(15) shows that rather different English expressions can be represented by the existential quantifier. The best way to read $\exists x$ in a logical formula

is 'There is an x such that...' or, to be more precise, 'There is at least one x such that...' The existential quantifier states that at least one member of the universe of discourse satisfies the open sentence that follows the quantifier.

The logical formulas in (15) would read as follows.

(16)   (a)   There is at least one x such that x is conservative
        (b)   There is at least one x such that x is a unicorn
        (c)   There is at least one x such that x is a girl and such that x is nicer than Jane

Since the sentences in (16) are symbol-by-symbol 'retranslations' of the formulas in (15) into English, they sound somewhat clumsy.

The universal and the existential quantifier function differently in some respects. One thing that seems strange to a beginner in logic is the way in which the following two English sentences are represented.

(17)   Every girl is pretty $\forall x\,(G(x) \to P(x))$
(18)   Some girl is pretty $\exists x\,(G(x)\ \&\ P(x))$

The only difference between (17) and (18) seems to be that they contain different quantifiers. Looking at the logical representations of these sentences, however, we see that not only do they have different quantifiers in them but they also contain different logical connectives. This may look strange at first, but it is easy to show that it would be impossible to exchange the logical connectives in (17) and (18).

The logical representation of (17) contains an implication. If this implication is changed to a conjunction, we get (19).

(19) $\forall x\,(G(x)\ \&\ P(x))$

(19) says that every individual in the universe of discourse is both a girl and pretty. Hence, (17) and (19) are not equivalent. (17) does not exclude the possibility of there being some ugly boys in the universe of discourse, as does (19). This means that (19) is not a correct representation of the meaning of sentence (17).

(18) contains a conjunction. If this conjunction is changed to an implication, we get (20).

(20) $\exists x\,(G(x) \to P(x))$

(20) says that there is at least one x in the universe of discourse such that if that x were a girl, that x would be pretty. (20) becomes true if

some object that is not a girl is found in the universe of discourse (because of the facts of the material implication that is used in logic). (18) would not become true under such circumstances. Furthermore, (20) does not imply that there exists any girl in the universe of discourse, whereas (18) does. This shows that (18) and (20) are not equivalent and that (20) is an incorrect representation of the meaning of (18).

From a linguistic point of view, the two logical representations (17) and (18) are both somewhat counterintuitive. (21) and (22) give linguistically more satisfying representations of sentences (17) and (18).

(21) $\forall x$ $P(x)$ 'For every girl x, it holds that x is pretty'
         $x \in G$

(22) $\exists x$ $P(x)$ 'For some girl x, it holds that x is pretty'
         $x \in G$

In these formulas, we have what is usually called **restricted quantification**. The expression below the quantifier indicates the range of the quantification – in this case, the set of all girls. G stands for the set of all girls and $\in$ is the element relation of set theory. (21) and (22) show the parallel between the two sentences that (17) and (18) did not show. The only difference between (21) and (22) lies in the choice of quantifier, and by writing the range of the quantification as a subscript, we avoid using different connectives in the formulas. Restricted quantification is not standard in logic but could be included to give a more adequate analysis of natural language.

We can have more than one quantifier in the same logical formula. Thus, (23) is a well-formed expression of predicate logic.

(23) $\forall x \, \exists y \, \forall z \, R(x, y, z)$

The order of quantifiers is not arbitrary when more than one precedes the open sentence, since the order indicates their scope with respect to each other.

Compare the following two formulas, where $F(x, y)$ stands for 'x is the father of y'.

(24) $\forall y \, \exists x \, F(x, y)$ 'For every y, it holds that there is an x such that x is the father of y'

(25) $\exists x \, \forall y \, F(x, y)$ 'There is an x such that it holds for every y that x is the father of y'

The only difference between the two sentences is that the existential quantifier is within the scope of the universal quantifier in (24), while the reverse holds for (25). This fact influences the meaning of the sentences considerably. In plain English, (24) means 'Everyone has a father', which sounds reasonable. On the other hand, (25) means 'Someone is the father of everyone', which sounds far less reasonable.

In (24) it is said that no matter which individual we consider, it is always possible to find some individual who is his father. In (25) it is said that there is a cetain individual who is such that, no matter which individual we consider, the first individual is the father of the second one. This may sound complicated, but we will show below a way in which these differences can be illustrated.

There are sentences in English, like *Everyone admires someone*, for example, which are ambiguous depending on quantifier scope. The different readings of these sentences correspond to different formulas in predicate logic. The sentence mentioned has the following two readings. *A* stands for 'admire' in the formulas below.

(26) $\forall x \, \exists y \, A(x, y)$ 'Everyone has someone whom he admires'

(27) $\exists y \, \forall x \, A(x, y)$ 'There is someone whom everyone admires'

In order to see how quantifier scope works, let us consider a small universe of discourse with, say, only five individuals. Let us assume that the universe of discourse contains the individuals Alfred, Bruce, Charles, Dennis and Erod. The range of each quantifier is the set of these five individuals.

Let us consider (26) first. Under the quantifiers, we spell out the range of the variables. The dotted lines indicate that the first individual admires the second one.

(26′) $\forall x$ $\exists y$ $A(x, y)$

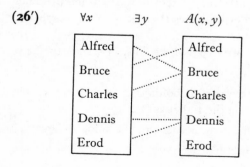

(26) says that it is possible to find one individual in the second set for each individual in the first set such that the first one admires the second one. The lines in (26') indicate this. Each of the individuals in the universe of discourse admires someone in the second one.

(27) is understood in a different way. This sentence says that it is possible to find someone in the universe of discourse who is admired by everyone, as is shown in (27').

(27') $\exists y$ $\forall x$ $A(x, y)$

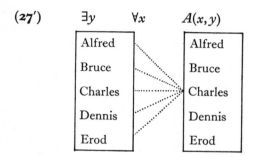

The difference between (26) and (27) can now be seen clearly. The important thing in (26') is that we find that for each individual in the first set there is some individual in the second set that he admires. The individuals in the first set may admire different individuals in the second set, but each of them must admire someone in that set. The important thing in (27') is that all the different individuals in the first set admire the same individual in the second set. As we see from (27'), all of them admire Charles.

A further point has to be made. (27) would still be true if for example Alfred admired Bruce in addition to admiring Charles. The important thing is that they all admire Charles.

Sentence (27) implies sentence (26), but (26) does not imply (27). This can be seen from the schema above. If everyone admires one and the same individual, it must be true that everyone admires someone. In other words, $\exists y \, \forall x \, F(x, y) \rightarrow \forall x \, \exists y \, F(x, y)$ but not $\forall x \, \exists y \, F(x, y) \rightarrow \exists y \, \forall x \, F(x, y)$.

The scope ambiguities produced by sentences containing two quantifiers are interesting from a linguistic point of view. Often intonation changes a potentially ambiguous sentence into a non-ambiguous one.

One example of this is the following line from a song that was popular some years ago: *Everybody loves somebody sometime*. If you know the tune, you will agree that this sentence can only be understood as having the universal quantifier with widest scope.

Another feature of quantifiers that has been discussed quite extensively in the linguistic literature is the following. The order that the quantifiers have in a sentence in English often corresponds to the order we give these quantifiers in the logical representation of the meaning of that sentence. Compare the following two sentences.

(28) (a) Everyone in this room speaks two languages
     (b) Two languages are spoken by everyone in this room

(28)(a) strongly favours the reading with the universal quantifier having the widest scope. (28)(b), on the other hand, favours the reading where the expression *two languages* has the widest scope. It may be that both sentences in (28) are ambiguous, but it is clear that the preferred reading in each case is the one where the logical representation has the same order for the quantifiers as the English sentence has. Since the passive transformation, which is used to relate (28)(b) to (28)(a), is thought of as a meaning-preserving transformation, these sentences create a problem for the linguist. Sentence pairs like (28) have been mentioned already in Chomsky (1957).

A similar problem is created by sentence pairs like the following.

(29) (a) Everyone did not explain the situation
     (b) The situation wasn't explained by everyone

What is important here is not the order of two quantifiers but the order of a negation with respect to a quantifier. For most speakers of English, (29)(a) is ambiguous and has the following two readings, where E stands for 'explain' and s for the situation.

(30) (a) $\forall x \sim E(x, s)$ 'For every x, it holds that x did not explain s'
     (b) $\sim \forall x E(x, s)$ 'It is not the case that it holds for every x that x explained s'

(30)(a) says that no one explained the situation. (30)(b) says that not everyone explained the situation – some did and some did not. (29)(a) has both these readings, but (29)(b) can probably only be understood as having the reading (30)(b). Yet (29)(b) is related to (29)(a) through the passive transformation.

With these examples, we leave scope ambiguities for the time being, but we shall have occasion to return to them in the chapter on modal logic.

So far, we have mostly discussed the syntax of predicate logic, i.e. how logical formulas are constructed in predicate logic. Before turning to the semantics of predicate logic, we will give a summary of the syntax.

5.3. Summary of the syntax of predicate logic

The purpose of the syntax is to specify which expressions constitute well-formed formulas of the logic. In this book, we treat propositional logic and predicate logic separately, but it should be clear that predicate logic contains propositional logic as a sub-part.

First we give a list of the categories of predicate logic.

(**1**) (a) individual constants $a, b, c, d \ldots$
  (b) individual variables $x, y, z \ldots$
  (c) predicate constants $A, B, C, D \ldots$
  (d) predicate variables $\Phi, \Psi, X \ldots$
  (e) sentence variables $p, q, r \ldots$
  (f) quantifiers $\exists, \forall$
  (g) logical connectives $\sim, \&, \vee, \rightarrow, \equiv$
  (h) parentheses $(\ )$

The formulas of predicate logic are built on this vocabulary. When the syntax of propositional logic was given, we introduced metavariables in speaking about sentences of the object language. Likewise, we introduce metavariables to speak about the expressions of the object language of predicate logic. The following metavariables are needed: P for predicate terms, $t_1, t_2 \ldots t_n$ for individual terms and $\alpha, \beta \ldots$ for well-formed formulas.

The following syntactic rules specify the well-formed formulas of predicate logic.

(**2**) (a) Every sentence variable is a well-formed formula
  (b) If t_1 is an individual term (constant or variable) and P is a one-place predicate term, then $P(t_1)$ is a well-formed formula
  (c) If t_1 and t_2 are individual terms and P a two-place predicate term, then $P(t_1, t_2)$ is a well-formed formula

(d) If $t_1, t_2 \ldots t_n$ are individual terms and P is an n-place predicate, then $P(t_1, t_2 \ldots t_n)$ is a well-formed formula

(e) If x is an individual variable and α a well-formed formula in which x occurs as a free variable, the $\exists x\, \alpha$ is a well-formed formula

(f) If x is an individual variable and α a well-formed formula in which x occurs as a free variable, then $\forall x\, \alpha$ is a well-formed formula

(g) If α and β are well-formed formulas, then (i) $\sim \alpha$, (ii) $\alpha\ \&\ \beta$, (iii) $(\alpha \lor \beta)$, (iv) $(\alpha \to \beta)$ and (v) $(\alpha \equiv \beta)$ are well-formed formulas

(h) A well-formed formula that does not contain any free variables is a sentence

(i) Only the formulas constructed in accordance with these rules are well-formed formulas

Note the difference between sentences and well-formed formulas. Both sentences and open sentences are well-formed formulas. The well-formed formulas constructed by rules (2)(a–d) are called simple or atomic expressions of predicate logic. The well-formed formulas constructed by rules (2)(e–g) are called complex expressions of predicate logic.

5.4. **The semantics of predicate logic**

To know the meaning of an indicative sentence is to know what the world has to be like for that sentence to be true. An English-speaker can decide whether the sentence *It is raining* is true in a certain possible world, if he knows what this world is like. This fact is the starting-point for logical semantics.

It is not sufficient, however – we also have to know how the terms of the language are related to the world. To know whether the sentence *Wotan is a god* is true in a certain possible world, we must know which individual the name *Wotan* refers to. If we have a language and decide how each expression of that language is related to the world, we say that we have an **interpretation** of that language. This language may be a formal language like predicate logic or a natural language like English. Next we will see how the expressions of predicate logic can be related to the world. Briefly, we can say that an interpretation relates the language to the world (or a possible world) by giving the extensions of the expressions of the language, i.e. the objects of the world that are designated by the expressions of the language (see the definition of the term 'extension' on p. 4).

Besides 'interpretation', the term **model** is often used, although this concept is usually introduced in a slightly different way. If a sentence is true in a certain interpretation, we may say that the interpretation **is a model of** the sentence. The kind of semantics presented in this section is often called **model-theoretical** semantics. (The word 'model' is used here in a way that differs from the way it is used in most scientific and everyday contexts.)

We start with the individual constants. To each individual constant, there corresponds a certain individual in the world. As an example, we take a language with the individual constants *a–h* and a possible world with the corresponding number of individuals. The individual constants are related to the world in the following way.

(**1**) a = Alfred e = Erod
b = Bruce f = Frank
c = Charles g = George
d = Dennis h = Harold

This constructed world contains these eight individuals and no others. In this case, we have a name for each individual in the world. This is a rather simplified example, which is constructed for expository purposes. It is considerably more problematic to give names to each individual in the real world, for obvious reasons.

Next we turn to the predicate constants. By the extension of a one-place predicate, we mean the set of individuals of which this predicate holds. The extension of a two-place predicate is the set of ordered pairs of individuals of which this predicate holds.

Briefly, we have the following situation.

(**2**)   (a)   A one-place predicate is interpreted as a set of individuals
  (b)   A two-place predicate is interpreted as a set of ordered pairs of individuals
  (c)   A three-place predicate is interpreted as a set of ordered triples of individuals
  ⋮
  (d)   An *n*-place predicate is interpreted as a set of ordered *n*-tuples of individuals

Let us introduce two one-place predicates, *M* for 'moose' and *C* for 'clever'. The following lists give the extensions of these predicates.

(3)   *M*:   {Alfred, Charles, Erod, George, Harold}
       C: {Alfred, Charles, Erod, George, Harold, Bruce, Frank}

The interpretation given here can be described in a diagram like (4).

(4)

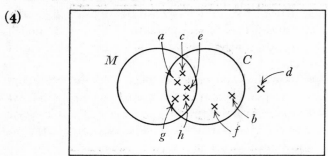

We can now take a couple of sentences and see what truth-value they receive in the given interpretation.

(5)   (a)   *M(b)*   'Bruce is a moose'   false
       (b)   *C(a)*   'Alfred is clever'   true
       (c)   *C(g)*   'George is clever'   true
       (d)   *M(e)*   'Erod is a moose'   true
       (e)   *C(d)*   'Dennis is clever'   false

The truth-condition for sentences of the form in (5) is simple and can be formulated as in (6).

(6)   A sentence of the form $P(t)$ is true in an arbitrary interpretation if and only if the object that is assigned to the individual term can be found among the objects assigned to the predicate in that interpretation

This means that $F(a)$ is true in a certain interpretation if the object assigned to *a* is included in the extension of *F*.

The truth-condition for a sentence with a two-place predicate can be formulated as in (7).

(7)   A sentence of the form $P(t_1, t_2)$ is true in an arbitrary interpretation if and only if the ordered pair of the objects assigned to t_1, t_2 can be found among the set of ordered pairs assigned to *P* in that interpretation

This means that a sentence $F(a, b)$ is true in a certain interpretation if the ordered pair of objects assigned to a, b is included in the extension of F.

Let us return to the interpretation described in (4) and see which of the following complex sentences are true in that interpretation

(8)　(a)　$M(g)$ & $C(b)$ 'George is a moose and Bruce is clever'　true
　　　(b)　$M(b) \lor C(d)$ 'Bruce is a moose or Dennis is clever'　false
　　　(c)　$\sim M(e)$　'Erod is not a moose'　false
　　　(d)　$M(b) \rightarrow C(g)$ 'If Bruce is a moose then George is　true

In determining the truth-value of these complex sentences, we start with the simple constituent sentences. In (8)(a), we find that both of the constituent sentences are true and that therefore the conjunction of the two sentences must be true. In (8)(b), we find that neither of the constituent sentences is true and that therefore the disjunction of the two must be false. The rules we follow here are identical to the rules of propositional logic. The only difference is that, in predicate logic, we start at a level below the starting-point for propositional logic. In propositional logic, the truth or falsehood of a sentence like $M(g)$ is taken as given, but in predicate logic we derive the truth or falsehood of this sentence from its internal structure.

In determining the truth-value of (8)(c), we start from the inside of the sentence and work our way out until we obtain the truth-value of the whole sentence. We start with the constituent sentence $M(e)$ and find that this sentence must be true since the object that e refers to is included in the extension of M in the interpretation given in (4). Next we consider the negation sign and find that $\sim M(e)$ must be false, since $M(e)$ is true, following the rules specified in the chapter on propositional logic.

Finally, (8)(d) must be true, since the first sentence is false while the second is true; this makes the implication true. A (partial) truth-table for (8)(d) is given in (9).

(9)　　　$M(b) \rightarrow C(g)$
　　　　　f　t　　t

In the discussion of the sentences in (8), we have illustrated how the rules of propositional logic enter into predicate logic. Let us now look at some complex sentences with quantifiers and determine their truth-values according to the interpretation given in (4).

(**10**) (a) $\exists x\, M(x)$ 'There is a moose' or 'Someone is a moose'   true

    (b) $\sim \exists x\, C(x)$ 'It is not the case that there is someone who is clever'   false

    (c) $\sim \exists x\, M(x)$ 'It is not the case that someone is a moose' or 'No one is a moose'   false

    (d) $\exists x \sim C(x)$ 'Someone is not clever'   true

    (e) $\exists x\, (M(x)\, \&\, C(x))$ 'Some moose is clever'   true

The principle here is that a sentence $\exists x\, F(x)$ is true in an interpretation I, if and only if F has at least one object in its extension in I. When this is known, it is simple to figure out the truth-value of the sentences with a negation in combination with the existential quantifier.

(**11**) (a) $\sim \exists x\, F(x)$ is true in I, iff the extension of F is the empty set in I

    (b) $\exists x \sim F(x)$ is true in I, iff there is at least one object in I that is not included in the extension of F in I

    (c) $\sim \exists x \sim F(x)$ is true in I, iff there is no object in I that is not included in the extension of F in I, which is to say that all objects are included in the extension of F

These truth-value definitions for combinations of an existential quantifier and a negation are redundant when the truth-conditions are given for the existential quantifier and the negation. They are given here for expository purposes. In both propositional logic and predicate logic, it holds that the truth-condition for a complex sentence is a function of the truth-conditions for the parts of that sentence.

With the interpretation given in (4) in mind, let us determine the truth-value of the following sentences.

(**12**) (a) $\forall x\, C(x)$ 'Everyone is clever'   false

    (b) $\sim \forall x\, M(x)$ 'Not everyone is a moose'   true

    (c) $\forall x \sim M(x)$ 'Everyone is not a moose; meaning 'For everyone it holds that he is not a moose'   false

    (d) $\forall x\, (M(x) \to C(x))$ 'Every moose is clever'   true

    (e) $\forall x\, (C(x) \to M(x))$ 'Everyone clever is a moose'   false

The main principle here is (13).

(**13**)   ∀x F(x) is true in I, iff all objects in I are included in the
                  extension of F in I

Let us spell out the details in full (14).

(**14**) (a) ∼ ∀x F(x) is true in I, iff not all objects in I are included
                                 in the extension of F in I, i.e.
                                 some objects in I are not in the
                                 extension of F
    (b) ∀x ∼ F(x) is true in I, iff all objects in I are not included
                                 in the extension of F in I, i.e.
                                 there is no object in the extension
                                 of F

Let us take an example from the sentences in (12). Looking at ∼ ∀x M(x),
we consider first the constituent sentence ∀x M(x), 'Everyone is a
moose.' We see that this constituent sentence is false in the interpretation
given in (4). Frank is not a moose in this interpretation, for example.
Since this constituent sentence is false, its negation must be true (i.e.
sentence (12)(b) is true).

From propositional logic, we know the truth-condition for the implication (see p. 38). Following this truth-condition, we give the following
truth-condition for sentences like (12)(d, e).

(**15**)   ∀x (F(x) → G(x)) is true in I, iff it holds for all objects
                                             included in the extension of
                                           F in I that they are also
                                           included in the extension of
                                           G in I, i.e. there is no
                                           object in F that is not also
                                           in G

5.5. **True in all interpretations**

Let us return to the inference with which we opened this
chapter on predicate logic. This inference is repeated in slightly modified
form.

(**1**)   Premises: All moose are clever
                          Bruce is a moose
          —————————————————
          Conclusion: Bruce is clever

For an inference like (1) to be valid or correct, it must be the case that it holds in all possible interpretations and not only in some particular interpretation; or, to use a somewhat different terminology: in all possible worlds where the premises are true, the conclusion must also be true.

If an inference is correct, it is impossible to construct a possible world where the premises are true while the conclusion is false.

How do we check that an inference is correct? Since there is an infinite number of possible worlds, it is not possible to go through all these worlds and see if the conclusion follows from the premises. By starting to go through the possible worlds one by one, we can only hope to show that an inference is not correct. The reason is that as soon as one interpretation is found that makes the premises true at the same time as it makes the conclusion false, we know that the inference in question is incorrect.

However, we may be able to show that an inference is correct. If an inference is correct, it is so by virtue of its logical structure independent of what the possible worlds are like.

The inference given in (1) is intuitively felt to be correct, and if it is correct, we should be able to show this by investigating its structure, as we said above. If an interpretation is found where the premises are true while the conclusion is false, we know that the inference is incorrect. If we can show that there is no such interpretation, we know that the inference is correct.

Let us now try to construct an interpretation where the premises are true and the conclusion false. We start with the first premise. What is needed for this premise to be true? Well, obviously, that all elements in the extension of the predicate 'moose' are elements in the extension of the predicate 'clever'. This situation is described by the diagram in (2).

(2)

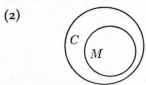

The second premise is true if and only if Bruce is an element in the extension of the predicate 'moose'.

(3)

When these two premises are taken together, we get the situation described in (4). We simply put (2) and (3) together in one figure.

(4)

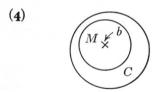

(4) describes what must be the case when both premises are true. In each possible world where both premises are true, it must be the case that the extension of 'moose' is a subset of the extension of 'clever' and that Bruce is an element in the extension of 'moose'.

If the inference in (1) is correct, it must be impossible for the conclusion to be false when both premises are true, i.e. when we have the situation described in (4). The correctness of the inference follows from the impossibility of constructing a possible world that makes the premises true and the conclusion false.

If the conclusion in (1) is true, Bruce is an element in the extension of 'clever'.

(5)

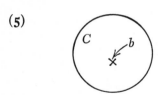

On the other hand, if the conclusion is false, Bruce is not an element in the extension of this predicate.

(6)

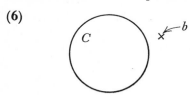

Of the two diagrams (5) and (6), only (5) is consistent with (4), which described what was necessary for the two premises to be true.

(6) is inconsistent with (4) because it claims that Bruce is not included in the extension of 'clever', but, since according to (4) Bruce is an element in the extension of 'moose' and since the extension of 'moose'

is a subset of the extension of 'clever', Bruce must be an element in the extension of 'clever'. In every possible world where (4) holds, (5) holds as well.

Hence, there does not seem to be a way of constructing a possible world where the conclusion is false when the premises are true, which means that the inference of (1) is correct.

We could have made this proof considerably shorter by using the formalism of set theory, but we have chosen to use an informal reasoning that uses the intuitions behind set theory instead.

That (1) is a correct inference does not mean that the sentence *Bruce is clever* is true in every possible world. It only means that this sentence is true in every possible world where the two premises of (1) are true. Consider the interpretation given in (7).

(7)

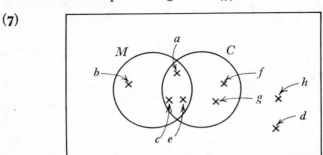

In this interpretation it is obviously false that Bruce is clever. Does this mean that (7) disproves that (1) is a correct inference? No; not at all. The reason is that in the world described in (7), it is not the case that both premises of (1) are true. The first premise, *All moose are clever*, is false in (7). As we see from (7), Bruce happens to be a moose that is not clever in that interpretation, so at least one moose is not clever.

Let us now turn to another inference which differs from (1) in that the conclusion and the second premise are substituted for each other.

(1)	Premises:	All moose are clever
		Bruce is clever
	Conclusion:	Bruce is a moose

Before continuing to read, you should ask your own intuitions whether this inference is correct or not. Not everyone's intuition gives the correct result immediately.

Now, is (8) a correct inference or not? Consider the interpretation described in (9)

(9)

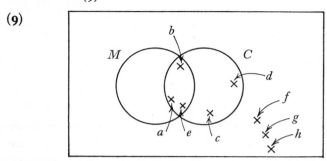

Both premises and conclusion are true in this interpretation. The first premise is true because the extension of 'moose' is a subset of the extension of 'clever'. The second premise is true because Bruce is an element in the extension of 'clever', and the conclusion is true because Bruce is also in the extension of 'moose'.

Does this show that (8) is a correct inference? No; we have only shown that the conclusion can be true when the premises are both true, not that it must be true when the premises are true. So let us try to construct an interpretation in which the premises are true and the conclusion false.

For the first premise to be true, the extension of 'moose' must be a subset of the extension of 'clever'.

(10)

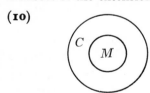

The second premise is true only if Bruce is an element in the extension of 'clever'.

(11)

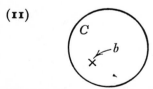

Now there are two ways of combining (10) and (11). These are shown in (12)(a) and (12)(b).

(12) (a) (b)

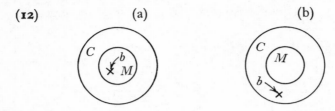

In all the worlds where (12)(a) or (12)(b) obtains, it is the case that both premises are true; but the conclusion of (8) is consistent only with (12)(a), not with (12)(b). The conclusion is true only when Bruce is an element in the extension of 'moose'.

One of the possible worlds in which the situation given in (12)(b) holds is that which is described by the interpretation in (13).

(13)

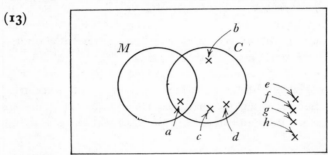

(13) shows that there is at least one possible world in which the premises are true while the conclusion is false. This means that (8) is not a correct inference.

In the discussion of the quantifiers above, you may have noted that a sentence with a universal quantifier could be paraphrased by a sentence containing the existential quantifier and vice versa. In general a sentence with one of the quantifiers is always equivalent to a sentence with the other quantifier. Thus the sentences in (14) are true in all interpretations, which means that they are logical truths.

(14) (a) $\exists x\, F(x) \equiv\, \sim \forall x \sim F(x)$

(b) $\sim \exists x\, F(x) \equiv \forall x \sim F(x)$

(c) $\exists x \sim F(x) \equiv\, \sim \forall x\, F(x)$

(d) $\sim \exists x \sim F(x) \equiv \forall x\, F(x)$

We can illustrate the validity of (14)(a), for example, by informal reasoning. The first sentence in (14)(a) states that at least one element is within the extension of the predicate F, as (15) indicates.

(15)

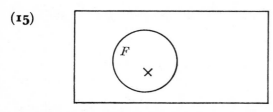

The second sentence in (14)(a), $\sim \forall x \sim F(x)$, is the negation of the constituent sentence $\forall x \sim F(x)$. This constituent sentence says that all objects in the universe of discourse are outside the extension of F, as indicated in (16). Obviously, the negation of this constituent sentence is equivalent to the sentence $\exists x\, F(x)$.

(16)

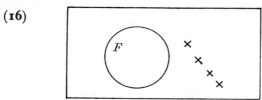

5.6. Summary of the semantics of predicate logic

In this summary of the semantics, we will use the same terminology as was used in the summary of the syntax. I will be a symbol which refers to an arbitrary interpretation.

(2)

   (a) $P(t)$ is true in I, iff t refers to an individual in I which is an element in the extension of P in I

   (b) $P(t_1, t_2)$ is true in I, iff $\langle t_1, t_2 \rangle$ refers to a pair in I which is an element in the extension of P in I

   (c) $P(t_1 \ldots t_n)$ is true in I, iff $\langle t_1 \ldots t_n \rangle$ refers to an n-tuple in I which is an element in the extension of P in I

   (d) $\forall x\, P(x)$ is true in I, iff all individuals in I are elements in the extension of P in I

   (e) $\exists x\, P(x)$ is true in I, iff there is at least one individual in I which is an element in the extension of P in I

   (f) $\sim \alpha$ is true in I, iff α is not true in I

   (g) $\alpha\ \&\ \beta$ is true in I, iff both α and β are true in I

(h) $\alpha \lor \beta$ is true in I, iff at least one of the sentences α and β is true in I

(i) $\alpha \to \beta$ is true in I, iff α is not true or β is true in I

(j) $\alpha \equiv \beta$ is true in I, iff the two sentences α and β are either both true or both not true in I

These truth-definitions may look complicated at first glance, but once you have read sections 5.4 and 5.6 above, they should be fairly self-evident.

5.7. **A formal version of the semantics**

In discussing the semantics of predicate logic in section 5.4 and summing them up in section 5.6, we did not account for quantified sentences with two- and many-place predicates. The reason is that this is hard to do without introducing a technical machinery that may sound strange to a student with a non-mathematical or non-philosophical background.

Let us now introduce some of this technical machinery to see how more complex quantified expressions are interpreted. First, we introduce the set D, which is defined as the set of all individuals that occur in the interpretations, i.e. the set of all individuals in the possible worlds.

We can then construct the set S, which is defined as the set of all sequences constructed of the individuals in D. A sequence (see p. 12) can be regarded as an enumeration of individuals in D. The same individual may occur more than once in a sequence. Our friend Bruce may for example occur in ninth, twenty-seventh and ninety-eighth position in one and the same sequence. The ordered n-tuples in (1) all correspond to admissible sequences.

(1) (a) ⟨Bruce, Harold, Dennis⟩
 (b) ⟨Bruce, Bruce, Harold, Dennis, Bruce, Harold⟩
 (c) ⟨Bruce, Bruce⟩
 (d) ⟨Bruce, Harold, Dennis, Dennis, Dennis ...⟩
 (e) ⟨Harold, Harold, Dennis, Dennis⟩

Finally, we introduce f, which is called the **assignment function**. Informally, we can say that f determines the interpretations for us. To start with, f assigns a set of individuals to each interpretation. To interpretation I_n, f assigns the set D_n, which is intuitively the set of individuals that we can talk about in that world. This set is necessarily a subset of D, $D_n \subseteq D$. Some logics are so constructed that $D_n = D$, for any interpretation. This would mean that we find the same individuals in every possible world. Other logics are not restricted in this way. Intuitively, there seems to be no reason to introduce the restriction under discussion. The possible worlds differ from each other in a number of ways, and there does not seem to be any particular reason why they should not also differ in the set of individuals that they contain. These questions concerning the inhabitants of the possible worlds have been widely discussed in the literature.

Secondly, f assigns one individual to each individual constant in each interpretation. As you remember, such an assignment was also made in the more informal version of the semantics discussed above.

Thirdly, f assigns an extension to each predicate constant in each interpretation:

> to each one-place predicate in I_n, f assigns a set of individuals from D_n;
> to each two-place predicate in I_n, f assigns a set of ordered pairs of individuals from D_n;
> and so on.

Fourthly, f assigns an infinite set of sequences to each interpretation. To I_n, f assigns S_n, which is necessarily a subset of S. The set S_n is the set of all sequences that can be constructed from the members of D_n. Even if D_n contains a finite number of individuals, the set S_n is infinite because one and the same individual may occur at several places in a sequence. In what follows, we will speak about s as an arbitrary sequence from S_n.

In principle, an unlimited number of variables is allowed in predicate logic. We introduce the convention that the individual variables are $x_1, x_2, x_3 \ldots$ instead of $x, y, z \ldots$ This is just a notational convention which is of no importance whatsoever for the logic itself.

As was said above, s is used to refer to an arbitrary sequence in an interpretation. Let us introduce the following terminology. An expression like s_5 is used to refer to the individual in the fifth position in the sequence and s_i to the individual in the ith position of the sequence. At some places it will be more clear to write $s(5)$ instead of s_5 and $s(i)$ instead of s_i.

Using this terminology and the sequences, we will define truth in terms of the recursively defined notion **satisfaction**. In section 5.2, we said that an open sentence like $W(x)$ is satisfied by an individual Bruce if and only if Bruce walks. (It is important to note that an open sentence is not satisfied by a name but only by individuals.) The same notion of satisfaction will be used here, but we relate it to the notion of truth for sentences, i.e. formulas without free variables by the following postulate: A FORMULA IS TRUE IFF IT IS SATISFIED BY ALL SEQUENCES AND FALSE IFF IT IS NOT SATISFIED BY ANY SEQUENCE. This means that if a sentence is satisfied by one sequence, it is satisfied by all sequences.

In (2), we give the recursive definition of satisfaction in an interpretation. We say that a sequence satisfies a formula if the appropriate member (or members) of the sequence satisfies the formula.

(2) (a) s satisfies $W(x_i)$ in I_n iff s_i walks (where s_i is the individual in ith position in s and $W =$ 'walks')

(b) s satisfies $A(x_i, x_j)$ in I_n iff s_i admires s_j

(c) s satisfies $G(x_i, x_j, x_k)$ in I_n iff s_i gives s_j to s_k

– and likewise for other one-, two- and many-place predicates.

(d) s satisfies $\sim \alpha$ in I_n iff it is not the case that s satisfies α in I_n

(e) s satisfies $\alpha \vee \beta$ in I_n iff s satisfies α or s satisfies β in I_n

– and likewise for other connectives.

(f) s satisfies $\exists x_i\, \alpha$ in I_n iff there is at least one individual a in D_n such that s_a^i satisfies α, where s_a^i is the sequence obtained from s by replacing the individual $s(i)$ by the individual a

(Note that s_a^i denotes a sequence and not an individual as the similar expression s_i does.)

(g) s satisfies $\forall x_i\, \alpha$ in I_n iff for every individual a in D_n, s_a^i satisfies α, where s_a^i is the sequence obtained from s by replacing $s(i)$ by a

In this case every individual D_n can be inserted in place of $s(i)$.

The real advantage of this version of the semantics over the previous version (section 5.6) is what is said in (2)(f) and (2)(g), which enables us to handle sentences with more than one quantifier.

Let us see how this method handles a sentence with more than one quantifier. Consider sentence (3), where A stands for 'admire'.

(3) $\quad \forall x_3 \, \exists x_7 \, A(x_3, x_7)$

The steps in (4) below indicate what is required of a sequence for it to satisfy sentence (3).

(4) (a) s satisfies $\forall x_3 \, \exists x_7 \, A(x_3, x_7)$ in I_n

          iff for every individual a in D_n s_a^3 satisfies $\exists x_7 \, A(x_3, x_7)$

    (b) s_a^3 satisfies $\exists x_7 \, A(x_3, x_7)$ in I_n

          iff there is at least one individual b in D_n such that $(s_a^3)_b^7$ satisfies $A(x_3, x_7)$

          $((s_a^3)_b^7$ is identical to the original sequence s, except for the third and seventh position, where a and b occur instead. $(s_a^3)_b^7$ is obtained from s_a^3 by replacing the individual in seventh position by the individual b.)

    (c) $(s_a^3)_b^7$ satisfies $A(x_3, x_7)$ in I_n

          iff $(s_a^3)_b^7$ (3) admires $(s_a^3)_b^7$ (7), i.e. iff a admires b

    (d) Looking back at (4)(b), we see that s_a^3 satisfies $\exists x_7 \, A(x_3, x_7)$ in I_n

          iff some individual is admired by a in I_n

    (e) Looking back at (4)(a), we see that s satisfies $\forall x_3 \, \exists x_7 \, A(x_3, x_7)$ in I_n

          iff all individuals admire some individual in I_n

    (f) Since s was an arbitrarily chosen sequence, we can see that $\forall x_3 \, \exists x_7 \, A(x_3, x_7)$ is true in I_n

          iff all individuals admire some individual in I_n

(5) $\quad \exists x_2 \, \forall x_1 \, (A(x_1, x_2) \to D(x_2, x_1))$

Let us look at this somewhat more complicated sentence and see what is required for it to be true in an arbitrary interpretation I_n. We can distinguish the following steps.

(6) (a) s satisfies $\exists x_2 \, \forall x_1 \, (\dots)$ in I_n

          iff there is at least one individual a in D_n such that s_a^2 satisfies $\forall x_1 \, (\dots))$

    (b) s_a^2 satisfies $\forall x_1 \, (\dots)$ in I_n

          iff for all individuals b in D_n $(s_a^2)_b^1$ (1) satisfies $(\dots)$ in I_n

    (c) $(s_a^2)_b^1$ satisfies $A(x_1, x_2) \to D(x_2, x_1)$ in I_n

          iff $(s_a^2)_a^1$ (2) despises $(s_a^2)_b^1$ (1) when $(s_a^2)_b^1$ (1) admires $(s_a^2)_b^1$ (2), i.e. iff a despises b whenever b admires a

    (d) Looking back at (6)(b), we see that s_a^2 satisfies $\forall x_1 (\ldots)$ in I_n

          iff all individuals who admire a are despised by him in I_n

    (e) Looking back at (6)(a), we see that s satisfies $\exists x_2 \forall x_1 (\ldots)$ in I_n

          iff there is some individual who despises all individuals that admire him in I_n

    (f) Since s was an arbitrarily chosen sequence, we see that $\exists x_2 \forall x_1 (\ldots)$ is true in I_n

          iff there is some individual who despises all individuals that admire him in I_n

The method of substitution and the use of sequences are necessary tools when it comes to analysing quantified sentences with more than one quantifier. If you look back at the summary of the semantics of predicate logic as it was given in section 5.6, you will find there the truth-conditions for sentences of the types $\forall x\, P(x)$ and $\exists x\, P(x)$. However, the truth-conditions given in 5.6 do not help us when it comes to sentences containing more than one quantifier. With the mechanisms introduced in this section, we can handle sentences with more than one quantifier as well as pairs of sentences that differ only in the order of their quantifiers. Unfortunately, the techniques introduced in this section are rather complex, but it should still be possible to grasp the intuition behind the techniques, we think.

5.8. **Formal properties of relations**

    Two- and many-place predicates, when considered semantically, are called relations, and these can be divided into different types depending on their formal properties. We shall consider three parameters by which the dyadic relations (corresponding to two-place predicates) can be divided into different groups. These parameters are reflexivity, symmetry and transitivity.

5.8.1. *Reflexivity*

    If it is true of all individuals that they stand in relation R to themselves, $R(x, x)$, then R is said to be a **reflexive** relation. If no individual can stand in relation R to itself, R is an **irreflexive** relation. The following are definitions.

(1)   (a) $\forall x\, R(x, x)$

If this holds, the relation is reflexive.

(b) $\forall x \sim R(x, x)$

If this holds, the relation is irreflexive.

A relation which is not reflexive is said to be **non-reflexive**. 'As big as' and 'identical to' are reflexive relations. As examples of irreflexive relations, we can instance 'father of' and 'taller than'. A person may never be taller than himself or be his own father. 'Satisfied with' is a non-reflexive relation. A person may or may not be satisfied with himself.

5.8.2. *Symmetry*

If a relation R, whenever it holds between two objects x and y, also holds between y and x, the relation is said to be **symmetric** – i.e. if the relation always holds in the opposite direction. If the relation never holds in the opposite direction, it is said to be **asymmetric**. If a relation is not symmetric, it is said to be **non-symmetric**.

(**1**) (a) $\forall x \, \forall y \, (R(x, y) \rightarrow R(y, x))$

If this holds, the relation is symmetric.

(b) $\forall x \, \forall y \, (R(x, y) \rightarrow \sim R(y, x))$

If this holds, the relation is asymmetric.

The relations 'as big as' and 'has met' are symmetric, while 'bigger than' and 'father of' are asymmetrical. A relation like 'brother of' is non-symmetric.

If we look at sentence (2), we might think that 'brother of' is symmetric, but when we consider (3), we see that this is not the case. When a relation sometimes holds in the opposite direction and sometimes not, it is non-symmetric.

(**2**) Jack is a brother of Bill's
(**3**) Jack is a brother of Jane's

5.8.3. *Transitivity*

If a relation R, whenever it holds between both x and y and between y and z, also holds between x and z, the relation is said to be **transitive**. If this is never the case, the relation is said to be **intransitive**. A relation which is not transitive is said to be **non-transitive**.

(**1**) (a) $\forall x \, \forall y \, \forall z \, ((R(x, y) \,\&\, R(y, z)) \rightarrow R(x, z))$

If this holds, the relation is transitive.[1]

    (b) $\forall x\,\forall y\,\forall z\,((R(x, y)\ \&\ R(y, z)) \to\ \sim R(x, z))$

If this holds, the relation is intransitive.[1]

Relations like 'bigger than' and 'to the left of' are transitive relations, while 'father of', for example, is an intransitive relation. Most verbs like 'know', 'admire' and 'despise' are examples of non-transitive relations.

(2)   If Canute is as clever as Olaf and Olaf is as clever as Gunnar, then Canute must be as clever as Gunnar

All relations of the type 'as X as' are reflexive, symmetric and transitive. These relations are called **equivalence relations**.

5.8.4. *Converse*

    A relation R is said to be the converse of another relation S, if $R(x, y)$ is true whenever $S(y, x)$ is true. The relation 'parent of' is the converse of the relation 'children of'. A predicate in the passive voice can be regarded as the converse of a predicate in the active voice. For example, 'is seen by' is the converse of 'see'. Whenever it is true that Wotan sees Thor, it is also true that Thor is seen by Wotan.

The converse of a relation R is written $\check{R}$. If P stands for the relation 'parent of' and C for 'children of', we can say that $P = \check{C}$, i.e. 'parent of' is identical to the converse of 'children of'.

5.8.5. *Structure of the domain and co-domain of relations*

    Relations can also be classified according to how they relate domain and co-domain. Consider the two relations 'be father of' and 'be a full-time employee in'. There is a clear formal difference between

---

[1] In defining reflexivity, symmetry and transitivity, we have deliberately used a vague terminology. We have defined these concepts in the following way:
> If this (i.e. some formula) holds, the relation is said to be reflexive/symmetric/transitive.

There are two ways of making these definitions more specific:
> If this holds in an interpretation, the relation is said to be **extensionally reflexive/symmetric/transitive** (i.e. reflexive, symmetric or transitive in that interpretation).

> If this holds in every interpretation, the relation is said to be **intensionally reflexive/symmetric/transitive** (i.e. reflexive, symmetric or transitive in all interpretations).

This latter way of defining the concepts is the most interesting from a linguistic point of view. It means that the meaning of the predicate is such that the formulas defining reflexivity, symmetry or transitivity come out true in all interpretations. In giving examples of different kinds of relations in this section, we have used this latter and more interesting formulation of the definitions.

these two relations. Several persons can be full-time employees in one and the same industry, but several persons cannot possibly be fathers of one and the same child. On the other hand, one father can have more than one child, but one man cannot be a full-time employee in more than one industry. A relation like 'be father of' is called a **one–many relation**, and a relation like 'be a full-time employee in' is called a **many–one relation**. If the relation is of the type one–many, there corresponds to each element in the domain one or more elements in the co-domain, and to each element in the co-domain there is never more than one corresponding element in the domain. If a relation is of the type many–one, each element in the domain corresponds to no more than one element in the co-domain, and to each element in the co-domain there may well be more than one corresponding element in the domain. There are also **one–one relations**. A one–one relation has always one element in the co-domain corresponding to each element in the domain, and to each element in the co-domain, there is exactly one corresponding element in the domain. The relation between a person and his Social Security number is a one–one relation. Each person has only one Social Security number, and a certain Social Security number corresponds to no more than one person. The fourth type of relation in this classification is the class of **many–many relations**. An example of this type of relation is 'have read', as a relation between persons and books. One person may have read several books, and one book is mostly read by more than one person.

The following diagrams will make these concepts clearer. In each figure the domain of the relation is given on the left and the co-domain on the right.

(1)   One–many relation

        Ex.: 'be father of'

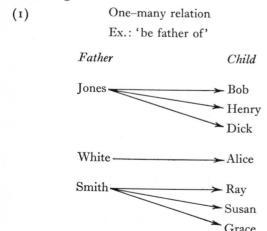

Father   *Child*

(2)   Many–one relation

Ex.: 'be a full-time employee in'

Person   *Industry*

Jones ————————————→ BMW

White
Smith ————————————→ IBM
Wilson
Johnson

(3)   One–one relation

Ex.: 'have the Social Security number'

Person   *Social Security number*

Jones ————————————→ 111-48-2257

White ————————————→ 231-13-7522

Smith ————————————→ 123-35-1234

Wilson ————————————→ 257-17-2579

Johnson ————————————→ 111-11-1111

(4)   Many–many relation

Ex.: 'have read'

Person   *Book*

Jones   *War and Peace*

White   *Tom Jones*

Smith   *Lady Chatterley's Lover*

Wilson   *Alice in Wonderland*

Johnson   The Bible

Many–one relations and one–one relations are called functions. The notion of a function has already been introduced in the chapter about set theory. For a relation to be a function, it has to be the case that each element in the domain is given no more than one element in the co-domain. This is the important restriction that is put on a function. It is easy to see that the set of functions is a subset of the set of relations.

EXERCISES

1. Let $a =$ Andy $\qquad A =$ admire
   $b =$ Burt $\qquad D =$ despise
   $f =$ Frank

   Translate the following expressions of predicate logic into idiomatic English.

   (a) $A(b, f)$
   (b) $A(b, f)$ & $D(f, b)$
   (c) $\exists x A(x, x)$
   (d) $\sim \forall x D(x, f)$
   (e) $\forall x (A(x, f) \to D(x, x))$
   (f) $\sim \exists x \forall y A(y, x)$
   (g) $\forall x \forall y (A(x, y) \to \sim D(x, y))$

2. Formalize the following sentences in predicate logic.

   (a) Canute is Danish
   (b) Canute was a liberal but Olaf was a socialist
   (c) No guy likes Lisa
   (d) Every student reads some book
   (e) No student answers all questions
   (f) If all students flunk, no student will be glad
   (g) You can if you try

3. Classify the following relations for reflexivity, symmetry and transitivity.

   (a) 'earn as much money as'
   (b) 'earn more or as much money as'
   (c) 'be a grandfather of'
   (d) 'fall in love with'
   (e) 'be a brother of'

4. Is the relation between a person and his fingerprint a function?

5. Give an example of

   (*a*) a many–many relation
   (*b*) a many–one relation
   (*c*) a one–many relation
   (*d*) a one–one relation

6. Give one example of a sentence in predicate logic that is false in all possible worlds.

7. Translate the following two sentences into predicate logic.

   (*a*) Roger saw a bear and Knut saw it too
   (*b*) Roger saw a bear and Knut saw one too

8. Formalize the ambiguity of the following sentence in the terms of pedicate logic.

   Everyone hates someone

9. Give two expressions in English that are related in such a way that one is the converse of the other.

10. Howis a two-place predicate extensionally interpreted in predicate logic.?

11. Formalize the following sentence in predicate logic.

   There is an' evil power

12. What is an open sentence?

13. Which of the following sentences are equivalent?

   (*a*) $\forall x(F(x) \rightarrow G(x))$
   (*b*) $\forall x(F(x) \mathbin{\&} G(x))$
   (*c*) $\sim \exists x(F(x) \mathbin{\&} \sim G(x))$
   (*d*) $\exists x \sim (F(x) \mathbin{\&} G(x))$
   (*e*) $\forall x \sim (F(x) \rightarrow G(x))$
   (*f*) $\sim \exists x \sim (F(x) \mathbin{\&} G(x))$
   (*g*) $\sim \forall x(F(x) \mathbin{\&} G(x))$
   Clue: look at p. 82.

14. Consider the following sentence, where *G* stands for 'girl' and *L* for 'like' and *a* refers to Archie.

   $\sim \exists x(G(x) \mathbin{\&} L(a, x))$

   (*a*) Give one interpretation that makes this sentence true.
   (*b*) Give one interpretation that makes this sentence false.

15. Consider the following interpretation.

a = Archie $\qquad\qquad$ c = Clary
b = Burt $\qquad\qquad$ d = Doris
B 'boy': $\{a, b\}$
G 'girl': $\{c, d\}$
L 'like': $\{\langle a,a \rangle \langle b, b \rangle \langle c, c \rangle \langle a, c \rangle \langle a, d \rangle \langle b, c \rangle \langle c, a \rangle \langle d, a \rangle\}$

Which of the following sentences are true and which are false?

(a) $G(a)$
(b) $\forall x L(a, x)$
(c) $\sim L(a, d) \vee \sim B(d)$
(d) $\sim \exists x G(x)$
(e) $\forall x L(x, x)$
(f) $\exists x \forall y ((B(x) \,\&\, G(y)) \rightarrow L(x, y))$
(g) $\forall x \forall y ((B(x) \,\&\, G(y)) \rightarrow L(y, x))$
(h) $\forall x \forall y \forall z ((L(x, y) \,\&\, L(y, z)) \rightarrow L(x, z))$

16. Consider the following interpretation.

a = Albert
b = Burt
c = Cuthbert
H 'horse': $\{b, c\}$
L 'like': $\{\langle a, b \rangle \langle c, b \rangle \langle b, b \rangle \langle b, a \rangle\}$

(a) Give one sentence that is false in the interpretation.

(b) Give one sentence with a negation which is true in the interpretation.

(c) Give one universally quantified sentence which is true in the interpretation.

(d) Give one existentially quantified sentence which is false in the interpretation.

(e) Give one sentence with both an existential and a universal quantifier which is true in the interpretation.

17. Construct an interpretation that makes all the sentences of exercise (1) above true.

6

Deduction[1]

6.1. The deductive system

In the chapters on propositional and predicate logic, we saw that certain sentences followed from other sentences (or rather propositions). When two sentences are related in this way we say that one sentence implies the other, and this relation is marked by the implication sign. In this chapter we are interested in the sentences that follow from other sentences whatever the world is like: we are interested in sentences that LOGICALLY follow from other sentences. That a sentence p logically implies a sentence q means that in every possible world where p is true, q is true as well. This can also be turned into a definition of logical consequence – the key logical relation:

(1) q is a logical consequence of p, iff there is no interpretation in which p is true and q is false.[2]

Here are two simple examples. The first (2)(a) is taken from propositional logic and the second (2)(b) from predicate logic.

(2)   (a) $(p \,\&\, q) \rightarrow (p \vee q)$
       (b) $M(b) \rightarrow \exists x\, M(x)$

The first example says that if both sentences p and q are true, then at least one of them is true. This is obviously true, and this truth can be proved by a truth table.

The second example says that if a certain individual referred to as b has the property M, then someone or something has the property M. This is also obviously true, and the truth of this statement is shown by the impossibility of constructing a world that contradicts this fact.

---

[1] A good treatment of the problems discussed in chapter 6 is found in Anderson and Johnstone (1962).

[2] Sometimes the notation $p \vdash q$ ('p turnstile q') is used for 'q is a logical consequence of p'.

It should be noted that in propositional logic, there is a formal method for deciding whether a certain sentence is logically true or not, the truth table. In predicate logic, there is no corresponding formal method. Instead, we have to struggle with inventing interpretations that make the sentences true or false.

A deductive system supplies a set of rules by which one sentence can be said to follow from another. In particular, we can show that sentences (2)(a) and (2)(b) are logical truths with the help of the rules of the deductive system. With a linguistic parallel, we can say that the rules of the deductive system form a 'grammar' for correct inferences.

Most rules of the deductive system have the following general form: given a sentence of type A, you may infer a sentence of type B. These rules must, of course, preserve truth – if the first sentence is true, the second must be true as well. We can say that the rules of the deductive system are meaning-preserving in the restricted sense of 'truth-preserving'.

What these rules will look like depends on the semantics, since the semantics give the truth-conditions for different sentence types. This is a minor point in this case, because we shall here only take up uncontroversial aspects of a deductive system.

We shall list below a set of rules from a deductive system. The rules should be understood in the following way: given a sentence of the form to the left of the slash, we can infer a sentence of the type on the right-hand side.

(3) **Conjunction Introduction**

$$p \Big/ q \Big/ p \mathbin{\&} q$$

This rule says that if we know that p is true and that q is true, we can infer the conjunction of them, $p \mathbin{\&} q$. This is self-evident but, nevertheless, useful.

(4) **Conjunction Elimination**

$$p \mathbin{\&} q \mathbin{/} p \quad \text{or} \quad p \mathbin{\&} q \mathbin{/} q$$

This rule says that if a conjunction of sentences is true, each one of the sentences is true.

(5) **Disjunction Introduction**

$$p \mathbin{/} p \vee q \quad \text{or} \quad q \mathbin{/} p \vee q$$

This rule says that if we have established the truth of a certain sentence, then we can infer a disjunction between that sentence and any other sentence.

With the three rules we have looked at so far, we can show that $p \vee q$ must be true when $p \,\&\, q$ is true. This is done in a deduction of the form given in (6).

(6) $p \,\&\, q$
         p (by Conjunction Elimination)
         $p \vee q$ (by Disjunction Introduction)

In a deduction, we show step by step how one sentence is inferred from another and by which rule this is done. Each line corresponds to one step in the deduction, and each step corresponds to the application of one rule of deduction.

(7)   **Disjunction Elimination**

$p \vee q$
$p \rightarrow r$ / r
$q \rightarrow r$

This rule says that if we have established the following three things, (i) the disjunction $p \vee q$ is true, (ii) p implies r and (iii) q also implies r, then we know that r must be true.

This rule is slightly more complicated than the preceding ones, but it should still be possible to grasp it intuitively. The rule can be tested in a truth table, if you should doubt its correctness. Since $((p \,\&\, q) \,\&\, r) \equiv (p \,\&\, (q \,\&\, r))$, we let & combine three sentences directly.

(8) $((p \vee q) \,\&\, (p \rightarrow r) \,\&\, (q \rightarrow r)) \rightarrow r$

```
t t t   t   t t t   t   t t t   t   t t
t t t   f   t f f   f   f t f   f   f t f
t t f   t   t t t   t   t f t   t   t t
t t f   f   t f f   f   f f t   f   t f
f t t   t   f t t   t   t t t   t   t t
f t t   t   f t f   f   f t f   f   f t f
f f f   f   f t t   t   f f t   t   t t
f f f   f   f f t   f   f f t   f   t f
```

A rule of deduction is just like an inference. The sentences on the upper left of the slash are the premises, and the sentence on the lower right of the slash is the conclusion. When we test an inference in a truth table, we put parentheses around the premises and conjunctions between them and then we put an implication sign between the set of premises and the conclusion.

(9)   **Double Negation Introduction**
$p \mid \sim \sim p$

(10)   **Double Negation Elimination**
$\sim \sim p \mid p$

(11)   **Equivalence Introduction**
$$\left. \begin{array}{l} p \to q \\ q \to p \end{array} \right/ p \equiv q$$

(12)   **Equivalence Elimination**
$p \equiv q \mid (p \to q) \,\&\, (q \to p)$

These last four rules are so obvious that no special comment should be needed. The correctness of each one of them can be tested by a truth table.

(13)   **Implication Elimination**
$$\left. \begin{array}{l} p \to q \\ p \end{array} \right/ q$$

This rule says that if we know that p implies q and that p is true, then we know that q must be true. This rule is usually called **modus ponens**.

The rules we have looked at so far say what conclusion can be drawn from a certain set of premises. To use these rules we need to have the appropriate premises. Otherwise the rules cannot be applied.

Now – and this is important – the deductive system supplies a rule or a method which allows us to reason without having any premises to start with.

Before we state this rule explicitly, we can give an example expressed in plain English.

(14)   Assume: Tom is taller than George
       Assume: George is taller than Jim
       In that case: Tom is taller than Jim
       Conclusion: If Tom is taller than George and George is taller than Jim, then Tom is taller than Jim

99

The reasoning in (14) seems intuitively sound. Note that we do not know anything about the height of Tom, George and Jim. We just assume that Tom is taller than George and that George is taller than Jim. From these assumptions we conclude that Tom is taller than Jim, because we know that 'taller than' is a transitive relation. From this reasoning we conclude the implicational statement at the end of the deduction. This conclusion remains true whatever the heights of Tom, George and Jim are. Whenever we derive a sentence from an assumed premise, we can deduce a conditional statement, the truth of which is guaranteed by the rule of **Conditionalization**.

A formal version of (14) is given in (15), where T stands for 'taller than'.

(**15**)

$$\begin{array}{ll} \lceil T(t, g) \,\&\, T(g, j) & \\ \lfloor T(t, j) & \text{by the transitivity of } T \\ [T(t, g) \,\&\, T(g), j)] \rightarrow T(t, j) & \text{by Conditionalization} \end{array}$$

The explanation of the line or bracket on the left of the deduction is: each time we introduce an assumption in a deduction, we mark it with a bracket. This bracket continues until the introduced assumption is discharged, which it is by the rule of Conditionalization. This rule is given in (16) under the name Implication Introduction, which will give us a terminology parallel with that of other logical connectives.

(**16**)   **Implication Introduction**

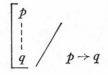

This rule says that if we can deduce q from p by some rules of the deductive system, we may infer $p \rightarrow q$ by the rule of Implication Introduction (or Conditionalization). Notice that p is not a premise in the deduction – it is only an assumption made for the sake of reasoning, and the validity of the inference does not rest on the truth of this assumption.

Another rule of some complexity is the rule of Negation Introduction. It is stated in the following way.

(17)   **Negation Introduction**

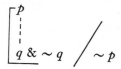

This rule says that if we can show that an assumption that we make leads to a contradiction, we are allowed to infer the negation of this assumption.

Let us illustrate this rule by an example. Consider first the following reasoning.

(18)   (a)   If it is night, Apollo is asleep
      (b)   Apollo is not asleep
      (c)   It is not night

This reasoning sounds intuitively correct, and it has the logical form of (19). This line of argument is referred to as **modus tollens** in the literature.

(19) $p \rightarrow q$
          $\sim q$
          $\sim p$

This inference can be tested by a truth table, but we can also derive the conclusion of (19) from its two premises in the deductive system. In doing this we make use of negation introduction.

(20)   (a) $p \rightarrow q$ premise
        (b) $\sim q$ premise
        (c) p assumption
        (d) q from (a) and (c) by Implication Elimination
                (i.e. modus ponens)
        (e) q & $\sim q$ from (b) and (d) by Conjunction Introduction
        (f) $\sim p$ by Negation Introduction

Negation Introduction indicates the way in which the method of reductio ad absurdum or indirect inference is introduced in the deductive system. When we want to deduce the conclusion (f) from the premises (a) and (b), we start by assuming the negation of the wanted conclusion. As we see, this assumption leads to a contradiction. This means that the negation of the conclusion (the assumption) is false, which in its turn means that the wanted conclusion must be true.

Next we will give two rules concerning quantifiers.

(**21**)   **Universal Instantiation** (first version)

$\forall x\, F(x) \;/\; F(a)$

This rule says that if we know that a certain predicate holds for all individuals, we may infer that it holds for each and every individual, e.g. *a*. Actually, rule (21) is not stated in terms that are general enough. The rule should rather say that whenever all individuals satisfy a given open sentence, each particular individual does. We may write this in the following way.

(**22**)   **Universal Instantiation** (second version)

$\forall x\, \alpha(x) \;/\; \alpha(a),$

> where $\alpha(x)$ means that x occurs free in α
> and where $\alpha(a)$ means that a has replaced all free occurrences of x in α

Example: consider the inference with which we started our discussion of predicate logic. In (23), we will deduce the conclusion 'Bruce is a moose' from the two premises of the inference, which are given on lines (a) and (b) of the deduction.

(**23**) (a) $\forall x\, (M(x) \to C(x))$
  (b) $M(b)$
  (c) $M(b) \to C(b)$ from (a) by Universal Instantiation
  (d) $C(b)$ from (b) and (c) by modus ponens

(**24**)   **Existential Generalization**

$F(a) \;\Big/\; \exists x\, F(x)$ or in a more general form $\alpha(a) \;\Big/\; \exists x\, \alpha(x)$

This rule says that whenever an open sentence is satisfied by a particular individual, e.g. *a*, then we can safely deduce that there is someone or something that satisfies the open sentence in question.

In the following deduction, we see some of the rules discussed at work.

(**25**)   (a) $\forall x\, F(x, b)$ assumption
      (b) $F(a, b)$ from (a) by Universal Instantiation
      (c) $\exists x\, F(x, b)$ from (b) by Existential Generalization
      (d) $\forall x F(x, b) \to \exists x F(x, b)$ from (a) and (c) by Conditionalization

With the help of Conditionalization together with the other rules of deduction we are able to derive all logically true sentences from an empty set of premises. From a logically true sentence, we can deduce other logically true sentences. From a contradiction, we can derive both all logically true sentences and all logically false sentences. This means that from a contradiction, anything follows. This may sound highly abstract, but it is interesting to note that natural language seems to have a construction that says just this.

(26)   If Canute drank tea, I'm the king of New Guinea

It is easy to show that any sentence follows from a contradiction. Take $p \mathrel{\&} \sim p$, which is an obvious contradiction. From this sentence we can derive an arbitrary sentence q. The reason is that the sentence $(p \mathrel{\&} \sim p) \to q$ can never be false. For this conditional statement to be false, it must be the case that the first sentence is true and the second one false. However, this may never happen, since the first sentence (i.e. the contradiction) is always false.

In connection with the rules of deduction, we can make some general remarks about so-called **axiom systems**.

An old idea is that every science should include statements of two types. The first type of statement is the **axiom**. An axiom is a sentence the truth of which is taken for granted. These sentences are intuitively true and they should be simple enough to provide a sound basis for the science in question. The second type of statement is the **theorem**. A theorem is a sentence that follows from the axioms by some rules of deduction. An area where axiomatization has been widely used is mathematics, and a good example of an area that can hardly be axiomatized is literary criticism. It is hard to imagine a set of axioms from which it can be inferred that the later dramas of Strindberg lack connection with reality.

Several attempts have been made to construct logic itself as an axiomatic system. A possible axiom in logic is **the law of the excluded middle**: $p \lor \sim p$. This law says that a certain sentence is either true or false and that no third alternative is possible. Many logicians take this to be an intuitively true sentence and accept it as an axiom for propositional logic. It should be noted, however, that not all logicians agree that this should be an axiom for logic (see below on the subject of presuppositions); therefore, they have to find alternative axioms. This means that we can speak about different logics. In modern times, some theorists have dropped the condition that the axioms should be intuitive (in geometry, for example).

Whenever theorems are inferred from axioms in whatever discipline, some set of deduction rules is always used. Next we will give a few examples that show that the rules of the deductive system are also used in our everyday natural language of reasoning.

6.2. Deduction rules in everyday conversation

In the previous section, we studied the structure and function of the rules of the deduction system in logic. In this section, we will see how these rules are used in the reasoning we perform in ordinary language. Very little has been done in this field, and no theory of reasoning in natural language exists in the actual world. It is to be hoped that such a theory will be present in a future possible world.

In order to study the role of deductive rules in natural language, we need to study the form of larger syntactic parts than sentences – we need a grammar of discourses rather than a grammar of sentences. The syntactic systems known today do not go beyond sentence level, but work is going on in this area, so the future may perhaps bring us the grammar of discourses that we need.

The only restriction that is put on the rules of the deductive system in logic is that they shall give rise only to valid inferences, i.e. when what is said on the left side of the slash in a rule is true, then what appears on the right side must be true, too. However, it is not clear that all the rules of the preceding section can comfortably be used in everyday reasoning. The following reasoning is 'logical' but nonetheless unacceptable in normal conversation.

(1)   A: I bought Russell's *Principia* today.

        B: Oh, I see, you bought Russell's *Principia* or Chomsky's *Aspects* today.

B's statement sounds rather infelicitous, even though he follows the rule of Disjunction Introduction. This does not show that Disjunction Introduction is never used in language. We have only shown that there the rule cannot be used indiscriminately to 'generate' discourses in everyday conversation. There might, of course, be other instances where the rule is used.

(2)   A: Do you think there will be a party tonight? q?
        B: I don't know, but one thing is clear: if Maja
            is at home, there will be a party. $p \rightarrow q$
        A: But Maja is at home. p
        _____
        A and B (merrily, in chorus): Then there will be
                                      a party tonight. q

As we see, modus ponens is used here.

Without having much evidence to fall back on, we claim that the method of reasoning which is called indirect reasoning in logic is used in everyday conversation. The following example illustrates this.

(3)   A: I think I will go and visit Knut.
        B: Knut is not at home. $\sim p$
        A: How do you know?
        B: If he had been at home, his car would be
            in the garage, but it isn't. $p \rightarrow q$
                                                           $\sim q$

In this example, we see something that is very common in everyday reasoning: not all steps in the reasoning are explicitly given in the discourse. A formal version of (3) would look like (4), and a formalized version of (4) is identical to the inference in (20) of the preceding section (6.1).

(4)   (a) If Knut is at home, his car is in the garage
        (b) Knut's car is not in the garage
        (c) Assume Knut is at home
        (d) Then Knut's car is in the garage
        (e) But we know that Knut's car is not in the garage;
               it leads to a contradiction to assume that Knut is at home
        (f) Hence, Knut is not at home

Another and very important fact about reasonings conducted in natural language is that we often do not state the premises from which we draw our conclusions. Consider the following example.

(5)   A: Mary has married a Swede.
        B: Oh God, Mary has married a polar-bear hunter.

It is easy to see that this conclusion does not follow from the premise given by A. For the inference to be correct, we must supply the following premise: 'All Swedes are polar-bear hunters.' Hidden premises like this one can be viewed as background knowledge shared by speaker and listener. (6) is a less categorical version of (5).

(6)   A: Mary has married a Swede.

           B: Hm. Mary has probably married a polar-bear hunter.

In this case, we have another hidden premise: 'Most Swedes are polar-bear hunters.' In everyday conversation, we often modify our conclusions by adverbials that express some degree of probability. On the basis of this, we can present the variables that play a role in this type of reasoning.

(7)   premises → qualifications → conclusion
                         ↑
           hidden premises
                 ↑
           background information (knowledge shared by speaker and listener)

The qualifications can be either of the 'probability form' that we saw an example of in (6) or of the type 'the conclusion follows unless this and that is the case', where situations are described in which the conclusion does not follow from the premises.

The point of this section has been to show that the rules of the deductive system might be a useful tool in analysing the reasoning that is conducted in ordinary language and vice versa, in describing and formalizing types of reasoning as yet not captured in formal deductive systems.

EXERCISES

1. Which rule of deduction permits us to deduce $\exists x Fx$ from $F(d)$?

2. Show step by step how $q \rightarrow p$ can be deduced from $p \equiv q$.

3. It must obviously be a valid inference to deduce p from the sentence p itself. However, there is no rule of the form $p \,/\, p$ in the deductive system as we have given it. Show how p can be deduced from p by the application of some of the rules given in chapter 6.

4. Consider the following deduction. Indicate after each line which rule has been used to infer that particular line.

(a) $(p \rightarrow q)$ & $(q \rightarrow r)$
(b) $p \rightarrow q$
(c) $q \rightarrow r$
(d) p
(e) q
(f) r
(g) $p \rightarrow r$
(h) $((p \rightarrow q)$ & $(q \rightarrow r)) \rightarrow (p \rightarrow r)$

5. Derive p from the two premises $p \equiv q$ and q by the rules given in chapter 6.

6. The following paragraph can be analysed as a deduction. Indicate how and by which rules the conclusion follows from the premises.

Gunnar was a Swede and he was a hero. All Swedes were drunkards and all heroes were murderers. Therefore, Gunnar was both a drunkard and a murderer.

7. Analyse the following reasoning in terms of the deductive system. Indicate which rules have been used.

Both Olaf and Gunnar were Vikings. Hence, it is not the case that Gunnar was not a Viking.

7
Modal logic

7.1. **Modal operators**

Propositional and predicate logics, as formulated in the preceding chapters, are restricted to talking of only one possible world at a time. When interpreting certain sentences in natural language, however, we seem to want to talk about relations between different possible worlds. We saw one example of this on p. 22. Another example is:

(**1**)   It is possible that it will rain tomorrow

A person who utters this sentence does not normally know for sure what the weather will be like tomorrow: he can imagine several possibilities. In other words, the world as it will look tomorrow is for him one of several possible worlds. What he says when uttering (1) is that there is at least one of these possible worlds where it will rain tomorrow.

The following sentence can be interpreted in a similar way.

(**2**)   It is certain that it will rain tomorrow (or perhaps, more idiomatically: It will certainly rain tomorrow)

(2) means that whichever of the possible worlds comes to be realized, it will rain tomorrow. In other words, it will rain tomorrow in all possible worlds.

We can thus define 'possible' and 'certain' in the following ways.

possible = true in some possible world
certain = true in all possible worlds

The possible worlds we talked about in these examples were more or less the worlds which are compatible with what we know. The logician is mostly interested in the worlds that are **logically possible**, i.e. all worlds which can be described in a consistent way, although they may be excluded by our factual knowledge about the world. For instance, in some logically possible world, you are not at this moment reading a textbook of logic for linguists but rather a sports magazine, although you would presumably not consider this a practical possibility.

What is true in all logically possible worlds is said to be **necessary** rather than just 'certain'. Concepts such as 'necessary' and 'possible' are studied in **modal logic**.[1] We can easily see the motivation for the choice of this term, if we realize that sentences such as (1) and (2) can be paraphrased with so-called **modal verbs**, e.g.

(3)   It may rain tomorrow

Other languages use the verbal category of **mood** (Latin: *modus*) in such cases.

Modal concepts are also expressed by sentence adverbs, such as *possibly, certainly*.[2]

Logicians use a formalism which is quite similar to the locutions we use in natural language. Two new logical constants, M and N, are introduced.[3] They can be put in front of just any sentence to yield a new sentence. Mp thus means 'it is possible that p' and Np 'it is necessary that p'. M and N are called **modal operators**. It is possible to iterate, i.e. repeat, modal operators and also to combine them with propositional connectives to obtain arbitrarily complex expressions, e.g.

(4) $MN \sim p \vee Nq$

There are certain logical relations between the two modal operators. They are illustrated by the following logically true sentences.

[1] The standard introduction to modal logic is Hughes and Cresswell (1968). Other works that treat semantic problems in modal logic are Hintikka (1969) and Rescher (1968). Further references are given below.

[2] For those readers who are familiar with probability theory, it may be worth while to point out that probability theory is founded on concepts which are fairly similar to those which underlie modal logic. The computation of the probability of, say, a certain outcome of a game of dice rests on the assumption that there are a number of equally probable possible combinations of single throws. Each such possible combination or outcome of the game is comparable to a possible world. Probabilities are usually graded from 1 (what is completely certain) to 0 (what cannot occur). In the terminology of modal logic, 1 is equal to 'true in all possible worlds' and 0 to 'true in no possible world'.

[3] There is a bewildering range of notational alternatives. Instead of M and N, some logicians use M and L, others $\Diamond$ and $\Box$, to leave aside other eccentric symbols that are sometimes found. In so-called Polish notation, which is introduced on p. 57, N is used for negation in propositional logic.

(5) $Mp \equiv \sim N \sim p$ 'It is possible that p iff it is not necessary that not p'

(6) $Np \equiv \sim M \sim p$ 'It is necessary that p iff it is not possible that not p'

In terms of possible worlds, we can rewrite (5)–(6) as (5')–(6').

(5') p is true in some possible world iff the negation of p is not true in all possible worlds

(6') p is true in all possible worlds iff the negation of p is not true in any possible world

From (5')–(6'), it is easily seen that (5) and (6) are really the modal logic counterparts of the logical truths formulated on p. 82, which were founded on the relations between the universal and existential quantifier. That there is such a connection between modal operators and quantifiers is one of the fundamental insights of logical semantics.

The modal operators may be added either to propositional logic or to predicate logic. In the first case, we obtain a system that can be called 'modal propositional logic'; in the second, a system that can be called 'modal predicate logic'.

7.2. Strict implication

In the chapter on propositional logic, we discussed the propositional connective →, 'material implication', which we read 'if ... then'. We mentioned that it does not quite have the meaning of *if* in English. For instance, if p is a false sentence, $p \to q$ is always true, irrespective of the truth-value and meaning of q.

This is hardly the case with *if* in English. For instance, (1) is not very likely to be interpreted as true.

(1)   If Sweden is in Africa, then Japan is a republic

The modal operators offer an alternative formalization of *if*-constructions. Suppose we simply add N to the left of the material implication.

(2) $N(p \to q)$

This would mean that $p \to q$ is true in all possible worlds – in other words, there there is no world in which p is true and q is false. We can interpret 'all worlds' either as 'all logically possible worlds' or 'all practically possible worlds'. In either interpretation, we could well conceive of Sweden's being in Africa without Japan's being a republic. Thus, if we choose to formalize (1) as (2), we might avoid some of the problems with material implication.[4] In modal logic, a connective $\dashv$ is often used which is defined in such a way that $p \dashv q$ (read 'p fishhook q') is equivalent to (2), where N is interpreted as 'logically necessary'. $\dashv$ is called 'strict implication'. Notice that strict implication is not a truth-functional connective: the truth-value of $p \dashv q$ cannot be computed from the truth-values of p and q.

We could also regard $p \dashv q$ as a statement about the truth-sets of p and q. If p is true only when q is true, the truth-set of p will be a subset (not necessarily a proper subset) of the truth-set of q.

7.3. **Other modalities**

A number of concepts other than those mentioned above have similar logical properties. Consider for instance the family of concepts having to do with obligations and permissions. These have been formalized in what is called **deontic logic**. Instead of the modal operators M and N, deontic logic exploits two **deontic operators** usually denoted by O (for 'obligatory') and P (for 'permitted'). Thus, Op, is read 'it is obligatory that p' and Pp'it is permitted that p'. These operators can also be interpreted in terms of possible worlds. The set of possible worlds considered here is the set of all 'ideal' worlds relative to some moral or legal system, e.g. the set of worlds in which everyone acts in accordance with the Ten Commandments. Op is then interpreted as 'true in all morally or legally ideal worlds' and Pp as 'true in some morally or legally ideal world'. The intuition is that a moral or legal system specifies a set of possible ways of arranging things: what is obligatory is what must be done not to go outside this set, and what is permitted is what can be done within this set. We see that the deontic operators are defined in a way which is more or less parallel to the definitions for the modal operators: what varies is only the character

---

[4] We have deliberately chosen to say 'avoid some of the problems', because there may still be some left. One problem that arises if we interpret *if...then* as strict implication is that when the *if*-clause is false in all possible worlds, the whole sentence must be true with such a formalization. For instance, the following sentence would be true, since the *if*-clause is logically false.

If *it* is raining and it is not raining, London is the capital of France

Perhaps this is not an entirely undesirable consequence. As we pointed out in section 6.1, one can use similar sentences to show the absurdity of a claim, as is illustrated by sentence (26) in that section.

of the set of worlds considered. It is not surprising, therefore, that logical truths in modal logic usually have exact counterparts in deontic logic. For instance, (5) in section 7.1 is paralleled by (1), which is also logically true.

(1) $Pp \equiv \sim O \sim p$

But there are also differences. Thus, since our own world is clearly a logically possible world but less obviously a morally ideal one, (2)(a–b) are logically true (if N is interpreted as 'logically necessary') whereas the deontic counterparts (3)(a–b) may well be false.

(2) (a) $Np \to p$
     (b) $p \to Mp$
(3) (a) $Op \to p$
     (b) $p \to Pp$

The close relations between deontic and modal concepts are also reflected in natural language. In almost all languages, the words and morphemes that are used to express certainty, necessity and possibility are also used for obligations and permissions (e.g. *must* and *may* in English).

As we said, modal logic and deontic logic differ mainly in the character of the worlds that are considered in the interpretation of the operators. Actually, this is true not only of these two kinds of logic: just by varying the conditions put on the worlds which are taken into consideration one may formalize a large number of concepts. In addition to 'logical possibility', 'practical possibility' and 'permissibility', one can think of 'modalities' such as 'physical possibility', 'conceivability', 'desirability', 'describability' etc.

Logicians use names formed from Greek roots to refer to concepts such as these, talking about **alethic logic** (which has to do with logical possibility), **epistemic logic** (which has to do with knowledge and belief) and even **boulomaic logic** (having to do with desire). In addition to being somewhat forbidding to outsiders, these terms may mislead by giving the impression that these systems are as different as propositional and predicate logic, whereas in fact, as far as syntax goes, they are almost identical, differing chiefly in the interpretation of the operators. In some cases, though, we arrive at systems that are also syntactically more complex than ordinary modal logic. For instance, we could formalize so-called **propositional attitudes** (beliefs, desires, hopes, fears etc.) by introducing subscripts on the operators that relate them to individuals with the attitude in question. For instance, in the system of epistemic logic formulated by the Finnish logician Jaakko Hintikka (see Hintikka (1962)), formulas such as $B_a p$ are used. This particular one means 'a believes that p'. In Hintikka's system, this is interpreted as 'in all possible worlds consistent with a's beliefs, p holds'. (See p. 62 for a discussion of this interpretation of propositional attitudes.)

An important concept in discussing different kinds of modalities is that of an **accessibility** or **alternativeness** relation. We can think of the set of possible worlds that we want to consider as defined by having a certain relation to our own or some other world. An important consequence of this way of viewing things is that the set may vary according to which world we take as the point of departure. To understand why this may be a desirable feature of the system, let us take the concept of 'conceivability' and interpret Mp as 'it is conceivable that p'. Suppose now that what is conceivable depends on the mental powers of the thinking creatures that happen to exist. Since in some other possible world there may be humans or other thinking entities that are more or less intelligent than those who exist in our world, it follows that what is conceivable in some world may not be conceivable in another. We will then say that each world has a set of worlds that are accessible from it via the conceivability relation, and that this set may vary from world to world.

Generally, then, each modality will correspond to a certain accessibility relation. Like all relations, accessibility relations can be characterized in terms of formal properties such as symmetry, reflexivity and transitivity (see p. 88). For instance, consider the differences mentioned above between logical possibility and permissibility. As we said, we live in a logically possible but not necessarily in a morally ideal world. This may be restated by saying that the set of worlds that have the accessibility relation to our world includes our world in the case of logical possibility but not in the case of moral permissibility. We can thus see that only the first accessibility relation could be reflexive (since in the second case, our world does not stand in the accessibility relation to itself).

Logicians have spent a considerable amount of time studying what follows if one supposes that accessibility relation has such-and-such properties. We can again refer back to our discussion of logical possibility and permissibility. The fact that (3)(a–b) are not logical truths is a direct consequence of the non-reflexivity of the deontic accessibility relations.

For those who want to read more about modal logic, it may be useful to know that the systems referred to in the literature as S4, S5 and T differ mainly in what properties are attributed to the accessibility relation, which has as a consequence that the sets of logical truths in these systems differ widely.

7.4. Problems connected with scope and identity in modal logic

7.4.1. *'De dicto'–'de re' ambiguities*
In the chapters on predicate logic, we discussed problems connected with the scope of quantifiers. In modal logic, scope problems are also important, perhaps more so than in predicate logic. There are two reasons for this. First, the number of operators is greater in modal logic, and there are consequently more possibilities of combining them in different ways. Second, when modal operators are combined with quantifiers, semantic problems arise that are important both from a general philosophical point of view and for the study of natural language. We could choose examples of scope ambiguities arising with the operators M and N, but it may be easier to understand some other cases, which involve propositional attitudes. We mentioned Hintikka's epistemic logic above (section (7.3), where $B_a p$ was interpreted as 'a believes p' or 'in all worlds consistent with a's beliefs, p holds'. Let us use the term 'a's belief worlds' to refer to the worlds consistent with a's beliefs. Consider now the following sentence.

(1)   John believes that all Nobel prize-winners are idiots

The problem here is that it is not clear what individuals John's belief concerns. It may well be the case that John is mistaken about the identity of the Nobel prize-winners. Suppose, for instance, that John has confused the professors Parsons and Pearsons and mistakenly believes that Parsons got the prize, when in fact Pearsons did. Let us further assume that John (correctly) considers Parsons a genius and Pearsons an idiot. In such a situation, is (1) true or false? On the one hand, if one asked John, 'Do you think all Nobel prize-winners are idiots?' he would answer 'No', since he believes that Parsons is a prize-winner and a genius. On the other hand, one could argue that it still may be true that John believes of all actual Nobel prize-winners that they are idiots. This might be more naturally expressed as (1').

(1′)   John believes of all Nobel prize-winners that they are idiots

In terms of possible worlds, the question boils down to the problem whether we are talking about Nobel prize-winners in the actual world or in John's belief worlds – in other words, how we determine the range of the *all*-quantifier in (1). The ambiguity in (1) corresponds to two different possibilities. To represent it in Hintikka's system:

(2)   (a) $B_a (\forall x \, F(x) \rightarrow G(x))$
       (b) $\forall x \, (F(x) \rightarrow B_a (G(x)))$

where F is 'is a Nobel prize-winner' and G is 'is an idiot'. Here the difference is in the relative positions of the universal quantifier and the belief operator. In (2)(a), the object of John's belief is the proposition represented by the formula $\forall x \, F(x) \rightarrow G(x)$. In Hintikka's semantics, this would mean that in all John's belief worlds, all Nobel prize-winners (i.e. the individuals that are Nobel prize-winners in those worlds) are idiots. In (2)(b), on the other hand, John believes a whole set of propositions, that is, for every Nobel prize-winner (who is a Nobel prize-winner in the actual world) he believes the proposition that this individual is an idiot. Using terms with a long tradition in philosophy, we can say that in the first case we have a '**de dicto**' modality; in the second, a '**de re**' modality. The motivation for these terms may be clearer if we take another example, involving not a universal quantifier but a definite noun-phrase.

(3)   John believes that the man who robbed him was red-haired

The critical case for the ambiguity in (3) is when John is mistaken about the identity of the man who robbed him. The definite noun-phrase *the man who robbed him* can be taken to refer either to the man who actually robbed John or to the man about whom John thinks that he robbed him. The first possibility would be the *de re* interpretation; the second, the *de dicto*. We can now better understand the terms *de re* and *de dicto*. *De re* in Latin means 'about the thing' and *de dicto* means 'about what is said'. In this context we should understand this to mean that in the *de re* case, what is important is 'the thing in the actual world', i.e. what the description refers to in our world, but in the *de dicto* case the important thing is what the description says about the object it refers to.

We have not yet shown how a sentence like (3) can be formalized. The treatment of definite noun-phrases like *the man who robbed him* –

so-called definite descriptions – is discussed in section 9.2 below. In order to be able to treat the ambiguity in (3) as a difference in the scope of modal operators, we have to use the so-called lambda operator, which is discussed in section 9.4.

7.4.2. *Specificity*

Ambiguities similar to those discussed above arise when operators expressing modalities are combined with existential quantifiers (or whatever corresponds to them in natural language). We shall choose an example with a deontic operator. Consider sentence (4).

(4)   John must talk to someone

The following contexts for (4) make clear that there are at least two ways of understanding it, if we assume that *must* is used deontically.

(5)   (a)   John cannot go on living like a hermit; he must talk to someone, or else he'll go mad
      (b)   John must talk to someone when he comes to London, but
he has lost the letter which says whom he must talk to

We see that only in (b) *someone* stands for a specific person in the actual world. In (a), we say that there must be some person that John will talk to, but it does not matter who this person is. In other words, every 'ideal world' contains at least one person whom John talks to, but it need not be the same person in each world. The following formulas will represent these two possible interpretations of (4).

(6)   (a) $O\,(\exists x\,T(a,\,x))$
      (b) $\exists x\,(O(T(a,\,x)))$
         where $T(a,\,x)$ is 'a talks to x'.

As we see, the difference is again in the relative positions of the operator and the quantifier. When the existential quantifier is outside the deontic operator, the formula entails the existence of an individual in the actual world, which is not the case if the positions are reversed. Linguists have referred to the two readings of (4) as 'non-specific' and 'specific' respectively. There is another way of understanding this term, however. It has been claimed that a sentence such as (1)(a) in section 5.2, repeated here as (7), is ambiguous.

(7)   Someone is conservative

The difference between the two interpretations would be that in one case the speaker would have a specific person in mind (whom he can identify), but in the other he would not. Opinions are divided about the nature of this ambiguity, but it seems clear that there is no natural way of rendering it within the systems of logic that we have discussed so far. Notice that it cannot be understood as a difference in scope, since there are no operators that can be ordered differently in a formalization of it.

Notice, further, that although we have shown in this section that certain ambiguities in English sentences correspond to unambiguous logical formulas which differ from each other with respect to the scope of operators, it does not follow that these ambiguities must be understood as scope ambiguities. Other explanations may well be possible.

7.4.3. *Opacity*

Closely connected with the *de dicto–de re* distinction is the concept of **opacity**. To explain what opacity is, we must first discuss a 'rule of deduction' that we can call 'substitution of terms with identical reference'. Consider the following inference.

(**1**) (a) Canute is red-haired

     (b) Canute is the King of Denmark

          (c) The King of Denmark is red-haired

Since the King of Denmark and Canute are the same person, it ought to be the case that whatever is true of one of them is true of the other. Therefore, it is generally possible to substitute the term *the King of Denmark* for *Canute* and vice versa without changing the truth-value of the sentence.[5] But there are cases where this principle seems to lead us astray. Consider the following (invalid) inference.

(**2**) (a) The King of Denmark could have been someone other than Canute

     (b) The King of Denmark is Canute

          (c) Canute could have been someone other than Canute

Clearly, (2)(c) does not follow from (2)(a), at least not if we take these sentences in their probably most natural interpretations, where (2)(a) says that it could have been the case that someone other than Canute

---

[5] Using a Latin phrase, we say that such terms are interchangeable **salva veritate**, 'with the truth unchanged'.

would rule Denmark – a perfectly natural thing to say – whereas (2)(c) says that it could have been the case that Canute would be non-identical to himself – something which appears to be logically contradictory. In other words, (2)(a) provides a context where it is not possible to substitute co-referring terms for each other. Such contexts have been called **opaque** contexts. (A context which is not opaque is called **transparent**.)

Which contexts are opaque and why? Notice that (2)(a) in the interpretation we mentioned is an example of a *de dicto* reading of a modal construction. Generally, it is the case that modal constructions create opaque contests for noun-phrases (in the *de dicto* reading). Sometimes the terms 'opaque' and 'transparent' are indeed used as synonymous with *de dicto* and *de re*. If we consider the interpretation of such sentences in terms of possible worlds, it should be clear why this is so. The identity statement (2)(b) above is about an identity relation in our world. In (2)(a), on the other hand, we are talking about some other possible world, and it may well be that the identity statement is false in that world. Another way of putting it is that (2)(a) is not a genuine statement about the real King of Denmark.

The crucial thing about individual terms in opaque contexts is that we must consider not only their extensions in our own world, but also their extensions in other possible worlds. We shall see in the chapter on intensional logic (chapter 8) that this can be made into an argument for the necessity of postulating, besides the extension of an expression, what is called its **intension**.

The term 'opacity' was introduced by Russell and Whitehead in their *Principia Mathematica*, but the origins of the notion can be traced back to the German mathematician Gottlob Frege's famous article *Ueber Sinn und Bedeutung* (translated as Frege (1952)). Frege noted that substitution of co-referring terms was not generally possible in indirect speech contexts (in the widest sense of 'indirect speech', including e.g. the complements of epistemic verbs like *know* and *believe*). He concluded that in such contexts, an expression does not have its usual extension (*Bedeutung*) but rather what he called its 'indirect' or 'oblique' (*ungerade*) extension, which he identifies with the intension (*Sinn*) of the expression. One of Frege's examples later became a classic and is usually referred to as the **Morning Star Paradox**. We can illustrate it with the following invalid inference, which is parallel to (2) above:

(3) (a)   Copernicus knew that the Morning Star was a planet
     (b)   The Morning Star is the same planet as the Evening Star

     (c)   Copernicus knew that the Evening Star was a planet

(*The Morning Star* and *the Evening Star* are different names for Venus.) Actually, the example is not an ideal one, since it is not perfectly clear that *the Morning Star* and *the Evening Star* do have the same extension: one could argue that they refer to different aspects or manifestations of the planet Venus ('Venus as it appears in the morning' and 'Venus as it appears in the evening').

7.4.4. *Cross-world identification*

We should also under this heading mention the problem of **cross-world identification**.

What does it mean to say that an individual, say Leif Eriksson, has such-and-such a property in another possible world? How do we know that the man in the other world is really Leif Eriksson, if he has quite different properties than the ones he has in our world? For instance, if I say

(1)   Leif Eriksson could have stayed at home and never discovered America

someone might object that if Leif Eriksson had not discovered America, he would be another person and it is therefore not meaningful to talk about what could have happened if he had not done so. Such questions have bothered many of those who have worked on the semantics of modal logic. Traditionally, it has been thought that properties are of two types: **essential** or **necessary** and **contingent** or **accidental**. If p is an essential property of Leif Eriksson, then Leif Eriksson has p in every possible world, or in other words, if something in some world does not have p, then it is not Leif Eriksson. If we knew which properties are essential and which are not, we would have no problems with cross-world identification. However, it is very hard to give any substance to the notion of an essential property – at least for individual objects; it may be easier for classes – and people have tried other solutions, but it would carry us too far to go into them here.[6]

[6] An excellent place to read more about these problems is Kripke (1972). One proposal that should be mentioned here is that of the American philosopher David Lewis (see Lewis (1968)). According to him, there are no identity relations whatsoever between objects in different worlds. Instead, an object in one world may have one or several **counterparts** in

7.5. **Counterfactual sentences**

We have already had occasion to mention counterfactual conditional sentences in connection with the discussion of material implication (p. 39). We also mentioned that strict implication (p. 110) might be a better 'translation' of the English subordinating conjunction *if* than material implication. However, in the case of counterfactual sentences, strict implication clearly is not adequate. Consider the following sentence.

(1) If John were Bill's brother, Bill would have six brothers (We assume that in the actual world Bill has five brothers)

If we translate (1) as $p \dashv 3 q$, it means that in all possible worlds where John is Bill's brother, Bill has six brothers. But this does not seem to be true, since there might well be possible worlds where some of Bill's real brothers are not his brothers or where Bill has seven or eight brothers.

Still, (1) seems to be a true statement given the circumstances. The intuition that we should capture is that in a counterfactual sentence such as (1) we are speaking about a situation which is as similar to the real situation as possible given that the *if*-clause is true. In other words, we are speaking about a world or worlds which differ from our world only by our making John a brother of Bill. A number of logicians (e.g. David Lewis (1973) and Robert Stalnaker (1968) have proposed theories which account for this intuition. They do so by introducing **degrees of similarity** between possible worlds. With the help of this concept, we can introduce an operator $-\square\!\!\rightarrow$ with the following interpretation.

(2) $p -\square\!\!\rightarrow q$ is true in a world W iff q is true in that world among the worlds where p is true which is most similar to W (In some cases, this rule must be modified by substituting 'those

> another world. In principle, those objects are chosen as counterparts which are most similar to each other. Lewis's idea was used by a linguist, George Lakoff (1970), in one of the first serious attempts to apply the notion of a possible world in linguistic semantics. Lakoff wanted to explain why *me* rather than the expected *myself* is used in a sentence such as the following.
>
>   I dreamed that I was Brigitte Bardot and that I kissed me
>
> Lakoff's hypothesis was that *I* and *me* in the last clause would both refer to counterparts to the speaker, but that these two would not in the world or worlds where they exist be identical to each other and the co-reference condition for the use of reflexive pronouns would thus not be met.

worlds' for 'that world', since two worlds may be equally similar to the actual world)

7.6. Tense logic and reference points

Consider these two sentences.

(1)   Two plus two is four
(2)   It was raining

(1) and (2) are different in one major respect. (1) is a true sentence whenever it is uttered, whereas the truth-value of (2) varies depending on when and where it is said. Actually, most sentences in natural language are **context-dependent** in some way or other,[7] that is, we must know something about the context in which a sentence is uttered in order to understand it properly. So-called **deictic** or **indexical** expressions are a familiar example of this. As we know, the reference of pronouns such as *I*, *we*, *you*, *this* and *that* and of adverbs such as *now* and *here* is determined by factors such as who talks to whom when and where. The expressions of predicate logic, on the other hand, do not exhibit any such context-dependence. Thus, if we look at the semantic rules for predicate logic, we do not find any reference whatsoever to the speech situation. A sentence is either true or false: the context in which it occurs has no significance.

Some logicians have wanted to construct systems that are more like natural language in this respect. They have suggested that the truth-value of a sentence should be determined only relative to a set of **reference-points** or **indices**, including e.g. the speaker, the addressee, the time of utterance, the place of utterance. Thus, (2) could be said to be true for, say, London at two o'clock on 23 May 1975.

A related feature of natural languages that logicians (notably the New Zealander Arthur Prior, in e.g. Prior (1957, 1967, 1968)) have tried to incorporate into their system is the category of tense. To this end, they have constructed what is referred to as **tense logic**. Tense logic is similar to modal logic, both in its syntax and in its semantics. Usually, one adds to the ordinary syntax of propositional or predicate logic a set of four temporal operators, for which we shall use the letters F, H, G and A, and which are interpreted according to the following rules.

(3)   (a) $F\alpha$ is true relative to a point in time t iff α is true relative to a point in time which follows t

[7] We are not referring here to the distinction between context-free and context-sensitive grammars.

(b) $H\alpha$ is true relative to a point in time t iff α is true relative to a point in time which precedes t

(c) $G\alpha$ is true relative to a point in time t iff α is true relative to all points in time which follow t

(d) $A\alpha$ is true relative to a point in time t iff α is true relative to all points in time which precede t

In the semantics of tense logic, points in time (or, if we like, the states of the world at each point in time) correspond to the alternative worlds of modal logic. The intuition is that we understand the expressions with tense operators by understanding what it would mean for the simple expressions to be true at other points of time. Perhaps the following simile will be helpful here. Imagine that some prolific film-producer made an enormous set of mammoth films, each of which would represent some alternative 'world history', and would consist of a sequence of frames, each of which would show the world as it was (is, or will be) at some point in time in some of these alternative world histories. It seems convenient to restrict the term 'possible world' to what we have called here 'alternative world-history', and use 'possible world-state' for the successive states represented by the frames. Notice now that if one lays clippings from several of the films side by side, the two dimensions differ: the vertical dimension in each film represents time, which is ordered, whereas the frames that happen to fall side by side do not correspond to any such ordering.

For any point in time, we can distinguish between the points that precede and the points that follow it. This makes it possible to have four operators in tense logic, whereas modal logic, where there is nothing that corresponds to the distinction mentioned, has only two.

In the same way as modal operators, tense operators can be iterated. For instance, we might get a combination such as the following.

(4) HAp 'It has been the case at some point in time that it had always been the case before that point that p'

As in modal logic, we also find scope differences of some significance in tense logic. For instance, consider the following sentence.

(5)   All people have been small children

This sentence has two interpretations, although one of them is factually absurd: either we want to say that for each person, there has been a time when he was a small child (which is true), or we want to say that there was a time when all people were small children (which is false). Tense logic offers us the following ways to formalize these interpretations.

(6) (a) $\forall x\, HC(x)$
     (b) $H\,(\forall x\, C(x))$

Here the ambiguity is interpreted as a difference in the scope of the operator H. However, in order to be able to interpret such formulas, we need to know exactly what the ranges of the quantifiers are. Otherwise, we would not know if we are talking about all people who exist now, all people who have existed at any time or all people who existed at some particular time or times in the past. The reader may want to try out for himself which of these possibilities make sense in (6)(a–b).

Similar ambiguities can be found with definite descriptions, e.g.

(7)   The Pope has always been a Catholic

with the two possible paraphrases in (8).

(8) (a) The person who is now Pope has always been a Catholic
     (b) It has always been the case that the person who was Pope was a Catholic

What are the relations between tense operators and the tenses of natural language? The operators F and H are sometimes referred to as the 'future operator' and the 'past operator' respectively. This terminology may be misleading, since it suggests that F and H would correspond to the future and past tenses of English. However, it is not possible to identify them with any single tense category of English. If we look at the (simple) past tense, for example, we can see that as it is normally used, it contains an implicit reference to a point or period in time that is given by the context. Thus, a sentence such as (2), repeated here, is slightly odd if the context does not make it possible to determine what point or period in time is being referred to.

(2)   It was raining

Within the system of tense logic we have presented here, such implicit temporal reference is not possible. One could therefore argue that a formula such as Hp comes closer to an English sentence with the present perfect, e.g. (9).

(9)   It has been raining

However, (9) normally has other implications, e.g. that the effects of the rain are still visible, which cannot be derived from the tense-logical formula. We thus see that a tense logic of the kind we have outlined here is much too crude to encompass the subtleties of English tenses, which does not mean, of course, that these subtleties are not amenable to logical analysis.

EXERCISES

1. What is the scope of N in the following expressions?

    (*a*) $N(\forall x F(x))$

    (*b*) $\forall x(N(\exists y(F(x, y))))$

2. Translate into modal propositional logic:

    It is necessary that it is snowing or it is not snowing

3. Translate into modal predicate logic and try to find out all possibilities to vary the scope of the operators, even if not all these possibilities are possible interpretations of this sentence.

    All students possibly read one book

4. Consider the following fallacious argument (adapted from Quine (1964)).

    George married Mary. Mary is a widow. Hence, George married a widow.

    What distinguishes this argument from the following correct one?

    George loves Mary. Mary is a widow. Hence, George loves a widow.

8

Intensional logic and categorial grammar

8.1. Intensions and extensions

In previous chapters we have shown how logical analysis parallels linguistic analysis. In this chapter we will attempt to integrate them into one theory.

In predicate logic, we gave meaning to linguistic expressions by correlating our language to a model in which extensions were assigned to individual constants and predicate constants, that is, single objects to individuals and sets of objects to predicates. In other words, providing a semantics for a language was taken to involve providing an account of which objects in the world individual terms and predicate terms should be taken to refer to. By doing this, we were, as a second step, able to formulate truth-conditions for the sentences of predicate logic. This, in turn, enabled us to characterize a notion of logical consequence for predicate logic and thereby to capture the kind of logical inferences that are possible in predicate logic. But many of the types of reasoning we normally engage in cannot be captured in the simple type of predicate logic we described in chapter 5. We have already discussed the addition of modal operators, and there is more to come. One of the things which were inadequate and oversimplified in our version of predicate logic was the conception of semantics as a simple pairing of linguistic expressions and objects in the world. It has long been realized that such a simple account of meaning, although perhaps necessary and desirable as a first step, is quite insufficient. One of the earliest arguments to show that such an account of meaning was inadequate to characterize certain interesting types of reasoning was provided by the Stoics. The example is a logical paradox (called the **Electra paradox**) designed to show that a simple referential account of meaning leads to absurdity and therefore cannot be correct (see the section on indirect inference). The scenario is the following: Orestes has returned home.

Electra does not recognize him, although she knows that Orestes is her brother.

(1)   THE ELECTRA PARADOX

    (a)   Premises: Electra does not know that the man in front of her is her brother

    (b)   Electra knows that Orestes is her brother

    (c)   The man in front of her is identical to Orestes

         Conclusion: Electra both knows and does not know that the same man is her brother

Similar examples have been provided many times through the ages; the medieval scholastics, Frege, Russell, Carnap and Church are just a few contributors. We discussed some such cases above under the heading 'Opacity' in the chapter on modal logic.

The usual way out of this type of paradox was indicated by the Stoics themselves. We must distinguish a third type of entity besides linguistic expressions and objects in the world – senses or concepts. (The Stoics used the term '*lecton*'.)

When we give an account of the meaning of a linguistic expression, it is not enough to relate it to an object or set of objects; we must also provide a sense or a concept for the expression. In a terminology which has become very generally accepted in recent years, we will in our subsequent discussion refer to the sense or concept related to an expression as its intension; and by the extension of the same expression, we will mean those objects in the world it refers to.[1] These concepts were earlier introduced on p. 4.

Let us first indicate the form of a solution to our paradox. The contradictory conclusion states that Electra both knows and does not know of a certain person that he is her brother. Now if we look more closely at the premises that led to this conclusion we find that in (a) and (b) we have used two different linguistic expressions to designate this person,

[1] The concepts intension and extension were originally used only in connection with so-called universal terms, i.e. terms that can apply to several different objects. Thus the word *tree* designates a large set of objects – its extension, by means of its intension, which could be described as the concept created through an act of abstraction over the properties that all trees have in common. See Kneale and Kneale (1962). Later, the distinction was generalized by Carnap to apply to singular terms as well. See Carnap (1947). The distinction now has roughly the same import as Frege's distinction between '*Sinn*' and '*Bedeutung*' (Frege (1952)).

viz. *Orestes* and *the man in front of her*. We also find intuitively that in spite of the fact that these two expressions refer to the same individual they do not have the same sense. In the terminology we introduced above, they have the same extension but different intensions. We now further suggest that this makes the proposition (see p. 20) that Electra is said not to know in (a) different from the proposition she is said to know in (b). Her knowledge in (b) pertains to the intension of the expression *Orestes* rather than its extension. This makes premise (c) irrelevant because it asserts only identity of extension. From knowledge of intension nothing really follows as far as extensions are concerned. Thus the conclusion is illegitimate.

Notice that the difficulties that force us to introduce intensions are dependent on the type of predicate we choose. If we had chosen some predicate like *kiss* or *kill* there would be no paradox (2).

(2) (a) Premises: Electra killed the man in front of her
     (b)   The man in front of her is Orestes
     _____
          Conclusion: Electra killed Orestes

Thus some predicates can be said to be **extensional**, while others like *know, realize* or *understand* are **intensional**. The two types of predicates differ from each other primarily in respect of what aspects of designated objects they focus on.

So intensions as well as extensions seem necessary if we are to understand more about language and reasoning. As we saw in chapter 2, the distinction between intensions and extensions could e.g. be used to explain the oddity involved in claiming that the set of female Presidents of the U.S.A. is identical to the set of all dogs that can write computer programs. The sets are extensionally equivalent, but the two expressions used to denote them have different intensions.

8.2. **Intension**

Next we will try to discuss how we should best conceive of intensions. Are they some kind of ideal abstract entities which somehow adhere to linguistic expressions? This view is referred to as conceptual **realism**, since its supporters believe that intensions (concepts) have real independent existence. Or, alternatively, are intensions some kind of mental ideas that people who use the expressions have? This view is usually simply called **conceptualism**. Or, finally, are they something totally different? One interesting proposal for an analysis of intensions was put forward by the logicians who developed modal logic (Carnap, Kripke, Kaplan, Montague).[2] They combined the elegance of a purely extensional semantics with some of the ideas in modal logic in order to treat intensions. Their idea was basically this: when we think of the intension of *female President of the U.S.A.*, we are really still thinking of extension but not of the extension in our world (i.e. the empty set). We are thinking of the extension the expression has in some possible world where the U.S.A. has a female President. The extension of an expression need of course not be the same in every possible world. My favourite dish may be Peking Duck in this world and Kentucky fried chicken in another, which would mean that the noun phrase *my favourite dish* had different extensions in the two worlds. From this it follows that even if two expressions happen to have the same extension in our world there is no need whatsoever for them to have this in some other world also. We can therefore, after all, differentiate *the female Presidents of the U.S.A.* from *the dogs that can write computer programs.*

But we are still not satisfied. What is it that all the various extensions of an expression in different possible worlds have in common? What is it that makes them all extensions of, for example, *red* and not *blue*? Our answer will be 'the intension', and in elaborating this answer we want at the same time to provide a tentative answer to another question which has bothered semanticists and logicians for a long time.

What is it that makes it possible for us to use language to speak about the world? How is it possible for me, by using the word *window*, to pick out a specific object in the world, not only for myself but for anyone who speaks the same language? In other words, what is the glue that ties language to the world?

The classical answer to this question is the **naming** or **labelling** relation. All linguistic expressions are really labels, and they name objects or sets of objects. The naming relation is supposed to be unproblematic, and the problem is just to show how everything in a language can be reduced to some kind of name. (This is basically what we did in our analysis of the semantics of predicate logic.) We will now suggest another approach. It is to use intensions as the kind of glue we were looking for to tie language to the world. An intension is something that relates a linguistic expression to its extension. It determines the extension of a linguistic expression. When we have knowledge of the intension of an expression, we therefore have a tool – or if we like,

[2] See Carnap (1947), Kripke (1963), Kaplan (1963), Montague (1974).

a principle – to pick out the objects in the world which it has as extension. In our previous terminology we can say that an intension is a function: something that for every possible situation or world picks out exactly those objects which make up the extension of a given expression there. By bringing in set theory and modal logic we can thus construe intensions as functions from possible worlds into extensions. To return to a previously posed question, we can therefore say that what the various extensions of an expression in different possible worlds have in common is that they are all values of an intensional function which for every possible world picks out exactly the relevant extension.

We can see that this analysis ties in well with what we said about the meaning of sentences on p. 47. We argued there that the meaning of a declarative sentence could, in an important respect, be identified with the truth-conditions of the sentence. The truth-conditions, in their turn, could be seen as a tool for deciding whether a sentence was true or false given a certain possible world – in other words, as functions from possible worlds to truth-values. If we take truth-values to be the extensions of sentences (a somewhat strange assumption, perhaps, but one which turns out to be just as good and much simpler than assuming the extension to be something like facts or states of affairs),[3] then this is exactly what we would expect the intension of a sentence to be. A proposition which is the usual designation for the intension of a sentence is thus a function from possible worlds to truth-values, while the intensions of predicates and individual terms are functions from possible worlds to sets of objects and objects respectively.

It is worth pointing out that this analysis of intension has made the concept essentially language-independent. An intension has extra-linguistic entities both as its domain (possible worlds) and as its range (objects and truth-values). Here again we are faced with the classic problem of deciding whether an intension is to be identified with the set of ordered pairs of its arguments and values or with real abstract timeless entities connecting worlds with objects and truth-values or perhaps, in the conceptualist view, with certain mental constructs. However we solve this problem we must somehow connect intensions with language.

---

[3] One of Frege's original reasons for this choice was that he could find no other object than the truth-value that would remain constant when extensionally equivalent terms were substituted in a sentence. A constant object was needed as the extension, since the extension of the sentence should not change if the extension of the terms in the sentence has not changed.

We do this by introducing a general interpreting function I which for every linguistic expression gives us the appropriate intension. We get the following general picture.

(1) $I\ (red) = \text{intension}_{red}$
       $\text{Int}_{red}\ (W_n) = \text{Ext}_{W_n}\ (red)$
       where:
       W_n = possible world with index n
       I = general interpreting function
       Int_{red} = the intension for *red*
       $\text{Ext}_{W_n}\ (red)$ = the extension for *red* in W_n

The general interpreting function picks out the intension for red (which is itself a function). The intension for red then gives us for any arbitrary possible world W_n the extension of red in that world. We can picture it diagrammatically as in (2).

(2)

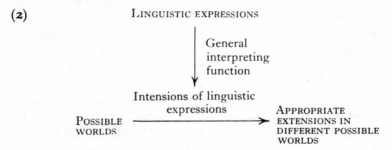

8.3. The Fregean principle

When we were discussing logical connectives we noticed that they had an important property in common – that of being truth-functional. That is, given any combination of truth-values for simple sentences (we take truth-values to be the extensions of sentences), the choice of connective completely determines the truth-value of the created compound sentence. In other words, they are entities that give us the extension of the whole as a function of the extension of the parts. This idea, which is sometimes called the **Fregean principle** (although there is some doubt that Frege actually formulated it explicitly), can be more generally formulated as follows.

> The meaning of a complex expression should be a function of the meaning of its parts

If for no other reason, this seems to be required if we are to explain how human language can be learned. As there seems to be no non-arbitrary limitation on the length or number of totally new sentences human beings can understand, it would, in view of the finite size of the human brain, be hard to explain how this is at all possible without some such principle as the Fregean principle. Of course we would not be helped if knowledge of an infinite number of functions were required in order to calculate the meaning of the whole from the meaning of the parts. Therefore we must postulate that some kind of recursion is involved, i.e. that we can apply the same operation (function) again and again to its own result, in the same way as the truth-functions designated by the logical connectives in principle are indefinitely reapplicable.

If to the idea that the meaning of a whole should be a function of the meaning of its parts we add the further idea that the syntax of language is fundamentally connected with the semantics of a language, i.e. that the syntax is a kind of map which shows how the meanings of the parts are to be combined into the meaning of a whole, and further add to this the analysis of intensions we presented above, then we arrive at the kind of semantic analysis of language which has been pursued within so-called **Montague grammar**. (The name derives from the American logician Richard Montague, who was the first to develop this type of grammar; see Montague (1974).)

It should be obvious to anyone who is familiar with the work of Chomsky and others on generative grammar that the position we have briefly outlined on the relationship between syntax and semantics is somewhat different from that taken by Chomsky. The position we have indicated here could be characterized as advocating 'isomorphism between syntax and semantics', while the position taken by Chomsky could be characterized as advocating 'the autonomy of syntax'. However, even if there is disagreement about the exact relationship between syntax and semantics, there is general agreement on the necessity of a recursive principle both in syntax and semantics.

Finally, it should be mentioned here that it is not clear what it would mean to apply the Fregean principle within the framework of a transformational grammar, since a sentence in this theory has not one syntactic structure but at least two (deep or underlying and surface). In fact, one could argue that one of the historic reasons for the introduction of the concept of deep structure was a desire for the existence of a level of syntactic structure to which the Fregean principle could apply (Fodor and Katz (1963), Katz and Postal (1964)). However, in Chomsky's most recent version of transformational grammar (the so-called extended standard theory), the Fregean principle clearly does not hold for the level of deep structure, since the semantic interpretation is also partly determined on other levels.[4]

8.4. The Fregean principle and categorial grammar

It turns out that what is usually referred to as **categorial grammar** provides a nice format for simultaneously achieving isomorphism between syntax and semantics and adhering to the Fregean principle, as well as making an intensional semantics possible. Categorial grammar was developed by the Polish logicians Leśniewski and Ajdukiewicz on the basis of some ideas put forth by the German philosopher Edmund Husserl. More recently work has been done by Yehoshua Bar-Hillel, Peter Geach and Max Cresswell.[5]

The basic ideas are these: if one wanted to be somewhat simpleminded about linguistic communication, one could perhaps describe it as involving essentially two things: (1) picking out some entity in the world; (2) saying something about that entity. The most typical way to pick out some entity is to use a NAME, and the typical way of saying something about that which has been picked out is to utter a SENTENCE. This is the starting-point of categorial grammar. There are only two basic categories, 'the bearers of reference and the bearers of truth' – the syntactical categories names (N) and sentences (S). Thus, by picking a name and then performing some kind of operation, i.e. 'saying something about it', we have produced a sentence. The formal way of describing an event of this type is to say that we have used the name as an argument for a function which produces the sentence as its value. Let us see what this involves in more concrete linguistic terms. What would be a simple way of producing a sentence from the name *John*? Well, one could, for example, add *runs* to the right of *John*, which would yield the sentence *John runs*. (In order to describe what happened we introduce the term **concatenation** for the process of adding linguistic expressions to each other right or left in linear order.) *John runs* was pro-

---

[4] This is so especially since some transformations seem also to affect truth-conditions, e.g. the passive.
[5] See Ajdukiewicz (1935), Bar-Hillel (1970), Geach (1972) and Cresswell (1973).

duced by right-concatenation of *runs* with *John*. We can say that *runs* is the mark of a function which right-concatenates the lexical item *runs* with a name to form a sentence. Such a mark could be called a **functor**. Thus *runs* is the functor of a function forming sentences from names. In fact, all intransitive verbs (IV) can be viewed as functors of such functions. More generally, a functor can be said to be a member of the set of linguistic expressions that correspond to a particular functional category.

So by using our two basic categories names and sentences as the argument and value of a function, we have been able to create a new category, viz. that of functions which map names into sentences. In categorial grammar, this category is designated S/N (the category which makes sentences out of names) and corresponds roughly to our old category of intransitive verbs. However, it is important to remember that while S, N and IV are categories of linguistic expressions, S/N is a category of functions. The expressions in IV are marks or functors for the functions in S/N. They are the lexical material on which the functions operate.

In principle there is no limit on the functional or derived categories that can be formed in categorial grammar. The general rule is:

(1)   If $C_1 \ldots C_n$ are categories then $C_1/C_2 \ldots C_n$ is a category

This means that forming categories is a recursive procedure. As $C_1 \ldots C_n$ are metavariables over categories we can always form a new category which maps any number of different categories onto any category. The format is very flexible. In fact, it allows for far more categories than one has any use for in linguistic analysis. An important problem in categorial analysis is therefore to choose exactly those categories which are linguistically relevant. Let us study some candidates for relevant categories. We can for example, create the category (S/N)/(S/N) corresponding to IV/IV. This category makes S/N from S/N. If we disregard the difference between S/N and IV, we can say that it makes intransitive verbs from intransitive verbs. What would the functors of this category be? Well, if we add *fast* to *runs*, which is S/N, in *runs fast* we still have an S/N, something which if added to a name would yield a sentence. So *fast* (taken in the sense of an adverb) is a functor of the category (S/N)/(S/N). In a tree-structure diagram *John runs fast* would look like (2).

(2)

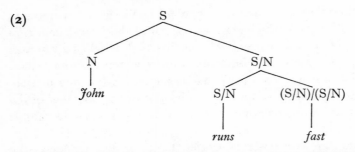

Other examples of derived categories would be S/S, S/SS. S/S is the category of functions making sentences out of sentences. *Necessarily*, *possibly* and other modal operators are all functors of this category. Consider (3) and (4) below.

(3)   It's raining

(4)   Necessarily, it's raining

S/SS makes two sentences into one sentence.

If we look at propositional logic, the sentential connectives can be viewed as functors of this category; p, q are mapped onto p & q. How would we describe English quantifier expressions like *someone* and *everyone*? They map predicates onto sentences, i.e. *runs* is made a sentence by the addition of *someone*, i.e. *someone runs*. Let us take predicates to be of category S/N – the category we have already assigned to intransitive verbs. This is reasonable in that by concatenating a name with a predicate we can produce a sentence. A quantifier should therefore be of category S/(S/N), something which makes sentences out of predicates. (There are other ways of construing quantifiers, however.)

Let us summarize what we have said so far by giving a syntax of a simple categorial language. A consequence of the fact that all derived categories are categories of functions is that we do not need any separate rules of formation. These are implicit in the categorial symbolism, i.e. if we know *or* is of category S/SS, we do not need a separate rule of the form S → S or S. This is implicit in the categorial symbolism.

However, the rules of formation are not fully implicit. The sequential ordering of the two S's in our example above is not determined. In order to determine things like sequential ordering (left- and right-concatenation) and inflection, we would either have to add so-called **spelling-out-rules** that spell out everything that is left undetermined by the categorial symbolism or we would have to complicate the categorial symbolism itself. J. Lambek in Lambek (1961) and John Lyons in Lyons (1968) suggest a step in the latter direction. Thus, Lyons uses $\overset{S}{\underset{N}{\leftarrow}}$ to designate an element that left-concatenates with a noun to form a sentence and $\overset{S}{\underset{N}{\rightarrow}}$ to designate an element that right-concatenates with a noun to form a sentence.

Since we are concerned with the principles of categorial syntax only in so far as they facilitate our understanding of intensional semantics here, we will be satisfied with the rather simple syntax we have been outlining above.

To complete our simple syntax, we only need to list the basic categories and those derived categories we find it useful to work with. Finally, we have to list for every category the **dictionary** (functor) **expressions** that belong to that category. This can be viewed as providing the vocabulary of the language. A word of explanation is perhaps needed here. Not every (functor) expression in a category is a dictionary expression; e.g. *runs* is a dictionary expression of S/N, but *runs fast*, though being S/N, is a derived functor expression. As the expressions that make up a sentence always derive from other categories, there are no sentential dictionary expressions.

(**5**)   A SIMPLE CATEGORIAL SYNTAX

	BASIC CATEGORIES	DICTIONARY EXPRESSIONS
(i)	S	none
(ii)	N	*Arthur, Canute, Tristan, Isolde*
	DERIVED CATEGORIES	
(iii)	S/S	*necessarily, possibly, not*
(iv)	S/SS	*and, or, if ... then, iff*
(v)	S/N	*runs*
(vi)	(S/N)/(S/N)	*fast, carefully*
(vii)	S/(S/N)	*someone, everyone*
(viii)	(S/N)/N	*seeks*

The category label of each functor set tells us what to combine it with and what the category of the resulting derived expression will be. *Seeks* (S/N)/N combines with an N like *Canute* to form an S/N *seeks Canute* which in its turn can combine with an (S/N)/(S/N) like *carefully* to form another S/N *seeks Canute carefully*. This can then be combined with another N like *Isolde*, yielding the S *Isolde seeks Canute carefully*.

(6) shows the derivation of *Isolde seeks Canute carefully* in a more succinct form. This time we will use a type of tree diagram, usually called an **analysis tree**, which is commonly used in Montague grammar.

(6)

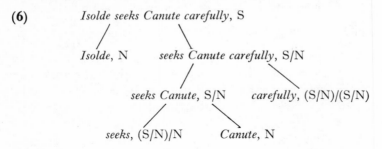

We see how each step involves the application of a function to an argument yielding as value the next higher step; e.g. we apply functions of category (S/N)/N to category N to get S/N. The formation rules which are implicit in the derived categories are therefore often called rules of **functional application.**

It should also be clear that the idea of construing all categories except S and N as functions has given us a very appealing way of realizing the Fregean principle. All complex expressions are formed by a step-by-step application of functions to arguments, thus making the final result a function of its parts. However, so far we have only shown that this is true for the syntax of the language outlined above. Our next step will be to show that it also holds for the semantics.

8.5. Categories, intensions and types

We would like our semantics to be intensional so that we can escape the kind of trouble we pointed out above in connection with the Electra paradox. We would also like there to be isomorphy between syntax and semantics. Finally, we want the Fregean principle to hold for syntax as well as semantics. Let us see how this can be done. The categories of syntax correspond in a one-to-one fashion to **semantic types** (we could have used the term 'category' here too, but this might create confusion). The basic semantic types correspond to the two basic syntactic categories sentences and names. The extensions of sentences are truth-values (extensional type t) and the extensions of names are entities (extensional type e). The intensions of sentences (propositions) are functions from possible worlds to truth-values. Such functions are indicated by $\langle s, t \rangle$, where s is a label for the intensional type corresponding to an arbitrary extensional type α. It generally holds that if α is an extensional type, $\langle s, \alpha \rangle$ is the intension corresponding to α. The intensions of names are functions from possible worlds to entities and are thus of intensional type $\langle s, e \rangle$. Such intensions are often called **individual concepts**.

Just as we did with syntax, we will now construct all the intensions and extensions of all other expressions on the basis of names and sentences. The extension of any derived type will be a function from the extension of one type to the extension of another. If we take *runs*, its extension will be a function from the extensions of names to the extensions of sentences. Consider the diagram in (1) showing how the extension of *John runs* is obtained.

(1)

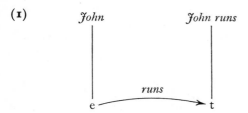

Instead of letting the extension of *runs* directly be a set taken from e, we are using the characteristic function (see chapter 1) from e to t, which picks out this same set as the extension of *runs*. By making the extension of *runs* a characteristic function, we can derive the extension of a sentence through functional application of *runs* to the extension of any name.

(2)   Ext (*runs*) (Ext (*John*)) = Ext (*John runs*)

What (2) says is: apply the extension of *runs* (a function) to the extension of *John* (an entity) and we get the extension *John runs* (a truth-value).

Based on the rule we gave for recursively forming derived syntactic categories, we can now give a rule for recursively forming derived extensional types.

(3)   If $C_1 \ldots C_n$ are categories and $E_1 \ldots E_n$ are the appropriate extensions corresponding to $C_1 \ldots C_n$ then the extension corresponding to a category $C_1/C_2 \ldots C_n$ will be a function from $E_2 \ldots E_n$ to E_1

Intensional logic and categorial grammar

By making the basic syntactic categories correspond to basic semantic types and the derived syntactic categories to derived semantic types through a recursive rule, we managed both to meet the requirement of isomorphism between syntax and semantics and the Fregean principle.

However, rule (3) gives us only extensions. As we wanted to make our semantics intensional, some more work remains. As we noted above, intensions can be seen as functions that for every possible world give us the extension of some linguistic expression. Thus $\text{Ext}_{W_i}(\alpha) = \text{Int}_\alpha(W_i)$ (the extension of α in world i is equal to the value of the intension of α for world i). As we have seen above, we can indicate the intensional type of an expression by prefixing s (for sense) to its extensional type. The intension of *runs* would thus be $\langle s, \langle e, t \rangle \rangle$. This should be interpreted as the function that for every possible world picks out the characteristic function of *runs*.

As we did with extensions, we can now provide a general recursive rule for forming derived intensional types.

(4)   If $C_1 \ldots C_n$ are categories and $E_1 \ldots E_n$ are the extensions that correspond to $C_1 \ldots C_n$, then the intension s which corresponds to $C_1/C_2 \ldots C_n$ will be a function from possible worlds to functions from $E_2 \ldots E_n$ to E_1.

If we use the rule to get the intension that corresponds to category (S/N)/(S/N) (which has adverbs like *fast* among its functors), we would get an intension that was a function from possible worlds to functions from extensions that correspond to S/N to other extensions that correspond to S/N. We could designate this intension in the following manner: $\langle s, \langle \langle e, t \rangle, \langle e, t \rangle \rangle \rangle$.

However, we have to complicate things a bit more to do justice to some of the intuitions that motivated us to introduce the distinction between intension and extension. According to the Fregean principle, the extension of a complex expression should be derivable from the extension of its parts. Let us therefore see what happens to the principle in an intensional context. We take individuals as the extension of names, sets of individuals as the extension of predicates and truth-values as the extension of sentences.

(5)   Bill is thinking of his future wife
(6)   Bill is kissing his future wife

There is one reading of (5) in which *think of* can be regarded as a relation between individuals. Sentence (5) would in this reading be true iff Bill and his future wife are to be found among the pairs of individuals who constitute the extension of *think of*. But there is another reading of (5) in which it can be true even if no individual in our world really is Bill's future wife (Bill might have died before he was old enough to marry). Bill could still have in mind the type of woman he would want for a future wife. This type of interpretation is completely impossible in (6), where Bill's future wife must exist in our world if the sentence is to be true.

But how are we to deal with the second reading of (5)? According to the Fregean principle, the extension of every complex expression should be derivable from the extension of its parts. But *Bill's future wife* needs no extension in our world in this reading. Can the Fregean principle be maintained? The solution we will adopt is the one Frege himself suggested. Some linguistic expressions (especially definite noun-phrases) in some contexts do not have what would normally be their extension as extension; instead they have what would normally be their intension as extension. The second reading of (5) provides us precisely with a context of this kind – a so-called **intensional context**. Sentence (6), on the other hand, provides a purely **extensional context**. This means that *think of* can provide both an extensional context (in the first reading, where it designates a relation between individuals) and an intentional context (in the second reading, where it designates a relation between individuals and individual concepts). So what *Bill's future wife* designates in the second reading of (5) is an individual concept, not an individual.

In the same way as names and definite noun-phrases, sentences can sometimes have what normally is their intension as extension; i.e. the proposition a sentence expresses can sometimes become its extension. This happens especially in contexts where a sentence is modified by a modal sentential adverb like *necessarily* or *possibly*.

(7)   Necessarily, it's raining

As we have seen, to be necessarily true means to be true in every possible world, not just in the actual world. *Necessarily*, therefore, does not operate on the extension of sentence (7) (its truth-value in our world) but rather on its intension (the proposition it expresses) which gives sentence (7) a truth-value in every possible world. *Necessarily* puts a condition on this truth-value. Thus, modal sentential adverbs, in an analogous way to verbs of the same type as *think of*, create intensional contexts where what normally serves as intension becomes extension.

In order to simplify these and other things, while at the same time capturing Frege's solution to the problem we are discussing, Montague (1974) suggested that one should generally complicate the extensions of all expressions in the following manner (what follows is a somewhat simplified version of Montague's proposal). In all contexts, names and sentences have as extensions individual concepts and propositions respectively. Out of context when they are isolated, they have as extensions their normal extensions. Since all other categories through their functional character are dependent on sentences and names, this means that all derived categories must also have their extensions altered. All expressions of derived functional category now have as their extension a function from the *intension* of the *argument* of the functional category (on the lowest level a name or sentence in context). Thus, expressions of category S/N now have as their extension instead of a function from e to t a function from type $\langle s, e \rangle$ to t. We therefore write the extensional type corresponding to S/N as $\langle \langle s, e \rangle, t \rangle$ and the intensional type as $\langle s, \langle \langle s, e \rangle, t \rangle \rangle$.

The intensions are thus obtained in the same way as before, only the assignment of extensions has changed. The extensions of functional categories are now always functions from intensions to extensions. We have, in a sense, hydraulically raised the whole system one step. Instead of starting from e and t in context, we now start from $\langle s, e \rangle$ and $\langle s, t \rangle$. Otherwise things are as before.

But we must give a new rule for the assignment of extension.

(8) (i) N corresponds to $\langle e \rangle$ and S corresponds to $\langle t \rangle$ in isolation (just as before)

(ii) If $C_1 \ldots C_n$ are categories and $E_1 \ldots E_n$ are the extensions corresponding to $C_1 \ldots C_n$, then the extension for $C_1/C_2 \ldots C_n$ is a function from $\langle s, E_2 \rangle \ldots \langle s, E_n \rangle$ to E_1, where s is the intension corresponding to an arbitrary extension E

This rule, in the same way as the one given in (3), will give us extensions for categories of arbitrary complexity. The difference is that we have now made it possible to have what was before the intension as extension. Just like our new extensions, our new intensions will be raised one step. The intension for category S/N is no longer of type $\langle s, \langle e, t \rangle \rangle$ but of type $\langle s, \langle\langle s, e\rangle, t\rangle\rangle$. But no new rule for intensions is needed. Given the new extensions, the old rule will do the trick.

What does the new assignment of extensions look like? Let us study the derivation of an extension for (9).

(9)   John runs fast

We will use both notation in type with angle brackets and a diagrammatic representation of what is going on. We start by characterizing the extensions and relevant intensions of the three words of the sentence: *John, runs* and *fast* (s = intensions, w = possible worlds, e = entities, t = truth-values; and the arrow signifies 'function from ... to').

(10)   *John*   extension: $\langle e \rangle$ ... intension: $\langle s, e \rangle$

(11)   *runs*   intension $\langle\langle s, e\rangle, t\rangle$ ... intension: $\langle s, \langle\langle s, e\rangle, t\rangle\rangle$

(12)   *fast*   extension: $\langle\langle s, \langle\langle s, e\rangle, t\rangle\rangle, \langle\langle s, e\rangle, t\rangle\rangle$

If one remembers the syntactic category of *fast*, which is (S/N)/(S/N), it becomes a little easier to analyse its type expression.

Let us now see how the interpretations of the simple expressions are combined to yield the interpretations of the complex expressions. First, the intension for *fast* $\langle s, \langle\langle s, \langle\langle s, e\rangle, t\rangle\rangle, \langle\langle s, e\rangle, t\rangle\rangle\rangle$ gives us its extension in our world $\langle\langle s, \langle\langle s, e\rangle, t\rangle\rangle, \langle\langle s, e\rangle, t\rangle\rangle$, which is the function we depicted in (12). This function is then applied to the intension of *runs* in accordance with (13). Remember that the arguments of derived types are always intensions. This gives us the extension of *runs fast*, which, just like the extension of simple *runs*, is of type $\langle\langle s, e\rangle t\rangle$. See (13).

(**13**)

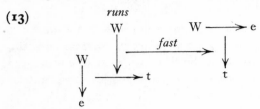

We now have the extension for *runs fast* in our world:

(**14**)

W
$|$
$\downarrow$ —→ t   or $\langle\langle s, e\rangle, t\rangle$
e

We apply the extension of *runs fast* to the intension of *John*, which gives us the extension of *John runs fast* (15) of type t, in other words a truth-value.

(**15**)   *John runs fast*

W
$|$
$\downarrow$ —→ t
e

We now compare the syntactic derivation of (9) with its semantic derivation in (16), in order to bring out the isomorphism between syntax and semantics.

(**16**) (a) Syntax:

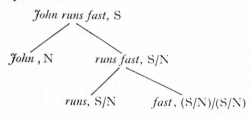

(b) Semantics:

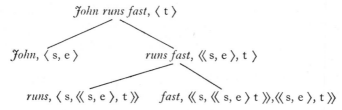

We can clearly see the parallelism between syntactic and semantic structure.

One might wonder whether all of these complications are really necessary. Would not a purely extensional semantics have been sufficient, after all? As we have seen, there are cases where this would be difficult. One such is the case with which we began the discussion – the Electra paradox. Electra knows something about the individual concept of Orestes, which is of type $\langle s, e \rangle$, not about his extension, which is of type $\langle e \rangle$. It would thus not be sufficient to treat *know about* as just a set of ordered pairs of entities with a characteristic function mapping them onto truth values. Rather it should be treated as a set of ordered pairs where each pair consists of an entity and an individual concept, i.e. a pair consisting of an extension and an intension.

We will consider two more examples that bring out the difference between a purely extensional treatment and a treatment which, like the present one, allows intensions as extensions.

(**17**)   Tristan seeks Isolde

In (17) Isolde need not exist in order for Tristan to seek her. *Seek* can therefore not be treated as a relation between individuals in a world. It is an intensional relation between individuals and individual concepts. Tristan is, via the individual concept of *Isolde*, seeking a world where *Isolde* has extension. The semantic analysis tree for (17) is given in (18).

(**18**)

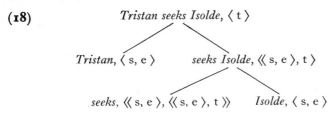

The extension for *seeks*, of type $\langle\langle s, e\rangle, \langle\langle s, e\rangle, t\rangle\rangle$, is applied to the intension of *Isolde*, of type $\langle s, e\rangle$, yielding the extension of *seeks Isolde*, of type $\langle\langle s, e\rangle, t\rangle$. The extension for *seeks Isolde* is then applied to *Tristan* $\langle s, e\rangle$, yielding the extension of *Tristan seeks Isolde* of type $\langle t\rangle$.

Using the kind of semantics we have introduced to handle intensional contexts, sentence (19) must be treated like (17).

(**19**)   Tristan kisses Isolde

This would be wrong, since *kiss* is an extensional relation between two existing individuals, which we have seen *seeks* and *think of* need not be. In order to maintain the difference between intensional and extensional predicates, one usually introduces rules that allow reduction of all extensional predicates to characteristic functions which are wholly extensional. Thus, *kisses* but not *seeks* could be reduced from type $\langle\langle s, e\rangle, t\rangle$ to type $\langle e, t\rangle$. Such rules are examples of what usually are referred to as **meaning postulates**. A meaning postulate, in general, is a rule or statement that regulates the interpretation of the terms in a language in a certain way, very often in the form of postulated equivalence or consequence relations between certain expressions of the language.

Let us now try to sum up some of the things we have said about categories, extensional and intensional types. We will do this by expanding a part of the simple categorial grammar given above with semantic information. (20) thus provides a fragment of a semantic grammar, where the correspondence between syntactic categories and semantic types is clearly indicated.

(**20**)   A VERY SIMPLE INTENSIONAL GRAMMAR

BASIC CATEGORIES	BASIC INTENSIONAL TYPE	BASIC EXTENSIONAL TYPE	EXAMPLES
S	$\langle s, t\rangle$	$\langle t\rangle$	
N	$\langle s, e\rangle$	$\langle e\rangle$	*John, Bill, Tristan, Isolde*

DERIVED CATEGORIES	DERIVED INTENSIONAL TYPE	DERIVED EXTENSIONAL TYPE	
S/S	$\langle s, \langle\langle s, t\rangle, t\rangle\rangle$	$\langle\langle s, t\rangle, t\rangle$	*necessarily, possibly*
S/N	$\langle s, \langle\langle s, e\rangle, t\rangle\rangle$	$\langle\langle s, e\rangle, t\rangle$	*runs*
(S/N)/(S/N)	$\langle s, \langle\langle s, \langle\langle s, e\rangle, t\rangle\rangle, \langle\langle s, e\rangle, t\rangle\rangle\rangle$	$\langle\langle s, \langle\langle s, e\rangle, t\rangle\rangle, \langle\langle s, e\rangle, t\rangle\rangle$	*fast, carefully*
S/(S/N)	$\langle s, \langle\langle s, \langle\langle s, e\rangle, t\rangle\rangle, t\rangle\rangle$	$\langle\langle s, \langle\langle s, e\rangle, t\rangle\rangle, t\rangle$	*someone, everyone*
(S/N)/N	$\langle s, \langle\langle s, e\rangle, \langle\langle s, e\rangle, t\rangle\rangle\rangle$	$\langle\langle s, e\rangle, \langle\langle s, e\rangle, t\rangle\rangle$	*seeks, kisses*

The extensions in the grammar are the extensional values of the intensions we have given. They are obtained by removing the first s of each intension. We can also give 'pure' extensions and get a semantics which would be very similar to the one we gave for predicate logic above. Such a semantics would be simpler but would not be able to handle the type of example that motivated the introduction of intensions. (21) gives a 'purely' extensional version of (20).

(21)

Category	Type	Ordinary designation
S	$\langle t \rangle$	sentence
N	$\langle e \rangle$	name
S/S	$\langle t, t \rangle$	one-place sentential adverb
S/N	$\langle e, t \rangle$	one-place predicate
(S/N)/(S/N)	$\langle\langle e, t \rangle, \langle e, t \rangle\rangle$	adverb
S/(S/N)	$\langle\langle e, t \rangle, t \rangle$	quantifier
(S/N)/N	$\langle e, \langle e, t \rangle\rangle$	transitive verb

This table would, except for the category (S/N)/N (transitive verbs), more or less correspond to the semantic types we used in our semantics for predicate logic. The price of achieving greater generality by introducing intensions is therefore considerably increased complexity. The difference in the treatment of transitive verbs is that whereas predicate logic regards transitive verbs, i.e. two-place predicates, as expressions that are combined with two terms to form a sentence (in categorial notation S/NN), we have here treated them as functors that together with one name form a one-place predicate. A transitive sentence is thus built in two steps: first we get *seeks Isolde* from *seeks* and *Isolde* and only then *Tristan seeks Isolde*. This has to do with the step-by-step construction of meaning and syntax through functional application.

So far, we have not given any truth-conditions. This can, however, easily be done. One would proceed in the following manner. *John runs* is true iff the extension picked out by the individual concept of *John* in our world is a member of the extension picked out by the intension of *runs* in our world. Truth is thus always defined relative to a world. Mostly our own world will be the relevant one. As this chapter has been intended as an informal outline of some of the ideas in intensional semantics and categorial grammar, we will not here give a formal semantics with truth-conditions.[6]

Finally, we should mention that our treatment differs from that which is common in Montague grammar in some respects. One such is the treatment of noun-phrases. Another is the way in which semantic interpretations are assigned to sentences. Instead of formulating a semantics directly for sentences in natural language, an indirect approach in three steps is usually applied. This has been prompted by the ambiguity and vagueness of natural language together with the formidable complexity that a direct assignment of semantic interpretations quickly leads to. The indirect approach is as follows. First natural language is regimented into what is called a disambiguated language (see also p. 167). Here every sentence is unambiguous (although not necessarily less vague). Then the disambiguated language is translated into expressions of intensional logic, and it is only at this stage that a semantics is finally given.

The reason for this procedure is that in intensional logic, we can create a model of natural language where we have everything under control, so to speak. We can then slowly approximate larger and larger chunks of the actual complexity in natural language. In this way, the complexities of natural language are taken care of by the translation rules rather than by the rules of semantic interpretation, which can be kept relatively straightforward.

This procedure has been fruitful in that it has made it possible to show, in a relatively simple manner, that the so-called deep structures of transformational grammar can be treated as a disambiguated language which can be translated into intensional logic and given a semantics of the type we have discussed here. See Cooper and Parsons (1976).

---

[6] For readers who are interested in this, see the works of Montague, Thomason and Partee in the bibliography.

Thus, the road has been opened for a unification of two of the most interesting theories today – Montague grammar and transformational grammar.

EXERCISES

1. Find two intensional verbs and two extensional verbs other than the ones given in the text.

2. Give a syntactic analysis tree for the following sentences using categorial grammar.
   (*a*) Bill runs and Mary sings
   (*b*) Bill runs on Saturdays
   (*c*) Bill kissed Mary hotly.

3. Give semantic analysis trees for the following sentences using intensional semantics and indicate if the verb permits reduction to pure extension.
   (*a*) Bill looks for Mary
   (*b*) Bill eats the fish
   (*c*) Bill eats the fish quickly
   (Treat *look for* and *the fish* as single terms)

9

Further extensions

9.1. Second-order predicate logic and predicate operators

Consider the following sentence.

(**1**)　　　John has an unusual property

A way to formalize sentences such as (1) is offered by the extension of predicate logic which is called **second-order predicate logic** (ordinary predicate logic is **first-order**). In second-order logic, it is possible for a quantifier to bind not only individual but also predicate variables. It is also possible for a predicate variable to be an argument of another predicate. The following formula, which would render the meaning of (1) is thus allowed.

(**2**)　　　$\exists \Phi \, (\Phi(a) \, \& \, F(\Phi))$
　　　　　where $a = $ 'John' and $F = $ 'unusual'

Second-order logic has been less well studied than first-order. Many textbooks do not treat second-order logic at all. We mention it here because it is sometimes suggested that it is useful for describing the semantics of various categories in natural language. For instance, the logician Hans Reichenbach proposed that adverbs such as *slowly* in *John drives slowly* should be regarded as second-order predicates (Reichenbach (1966)). Another proposal that does not entail such a radical extension of ordinary predicate logic is to treat adverbs as operators that form predicates out of predicates. If D is a predicate with the meaning 'to drive', there might be an operator S with the help of which we form a new predicate $S(D)$ 'to drive slowly'.

In a second-order predicate logic, one could also allow sentences to be arguments of predicates. This would mean that properties are predicated of propositions, which might offer a possibility of formalizing e.g. sentences containing *that*-clauses. For instance, a sentence such as

(3)   It is unbelievable that John will come

could be understood as saying of the proposition 'that John will come' that it has the property of being unbelievable.

9.2. **Presuppositions and definite descriptions**

It is usually assumed in logic that all sentences are either true or false. This is a practical assumption when constructing pure logical systems, but whether that makes sense for an adequate analysis of natural languages is disputable. Let us see where the problems arise. According to the semantics given above for propositional logic, $\sim p$ is true iff p is not true; in other words, the negation of a sentence is true whenever the sentence is false. But consider now the classical joke

(1)   Have you stopped beating your wife?

and the possible answers

(2)   Yes, I have stopped beating my wife

(3)   No, I have not stopped beating my wife

(3) appears to be the negation of (2). And if (2) is not true, (3) ought to be true. But a man who has never beaten his wife cannot answer either (2) or (3), since both answers commit him to having beaten his wife. We might then want to say that (2) and (3) in such a case are neither true nor false – that they have no truth-value whatsoever. It then follows that there is a condition for (2) and (3) having a truth-value, namely that the speaker must have beaten his wife at some time or other. Such a condition is called a **(logical) presupposition**.[1] Historically, this notion goes back to the German mathematician Gottlob Frege. In classical logic, presuppositions do not play any role, since all sentences are supposed to have truth-values, but it is quite possible to construct logics which permit sentences without truth-values – or which permit more than two truth-values – and where presupposition is an important logical relation.

We mentioned earlier (section 3.4) that propositions can be regarded as functions from the set of all possible worlds to the truth-values 'true' and 'false'. In a logic with presuppositions, one could regard these

---

[1] For accounts of the problems connected with the concept of presupposition, see Fillmore and Langendoen (eds.) (1971) (especially the articles by Garner and Keenan), Petöfi and Franck (eds.) (1973) and D. Cooper (1974).

functions as being defined (having values) only for a restricted set of worlds, namely those worlds where the presuppositions of the proposition are fulfilled. This set of worlds would then be the domain of the proposition.

There is also the alternative of introducing a third truth-value – 'zero' – in addition to 'true' and 'false'. A sentence with unfulfilled presuppositions would then have the truth-value 'zero'. In this analysis of presuppositions, a presupposition is a condition for a sentence to have a truth-value. If we interpret negation in the same way as in presuppositionless logic – in such a way that the negation of a true sentence is always false and vice versa – it follows that a sentence and its negation always have the same presuppositions. Indeed, this has been proposed as a test for presuppositions: if both a sentence p and its negation $\sim p$ can only be true when q is true, p presupposes q.

We can distinguish three important cases of presupposition in natural language: **existential**, **factive** and **categorial**. (There are also other types.) Examples of existential presuppositions are the following

Fafnir's car is red	PRESUPPOSES	Fafnir has a car
The University of Oxford is famous	PRESUPPOSES	There is a university at Oxford

Sentences which attribute a property to some individual object generally presuppose the existence of the object in question. Existential presuppositions are thus very frequent in natural-language discourses.

Factive presuppositions are exemplified by the following.

Ethelred regrets that Canute is clever	PRESUPPOSES	Canute is clever
It is strange that the earth is round	PRESUPPOSES	The earth is round

Factive presuppositions occur in sentences which contain predicates that express properties or relations involving facts. Such predicates are *regret, be strange, be astonishing*.

As an example of the third type of presuppositions, sortal or categorial presuppositions, consider the following sentences.

(4)   Fafnir is clever

(5)   The Eiffel Tower is clever

Is (5) true or false? We might claim that it is neither: the predicate *be clever* could be said to presuppose that its subject is something equipped with a mind. We can describe such cases in our logic by introducing the concept of domain also for predicates (earlier we talked of the domains of functions and propositions). Intuitively, the domain of a predicate is the set of all individuals of which it is meaningful to assert the predicate. The domain of *be clever* would thus be something like the set of all objects which can think (or have a mind). (It is important to keep this apart from the EXTENSION of *be clever*, which, as we know from the semantics of predicate logic, is the set of all objects which are actually clever.) The principle is then that a sentence $F(a)$ presupposes that a is in the domain of F. In the analysis where failure of presuppositions leads to truth-valueless sentences we would therefore get the three cases illustrated by (6).

(6)

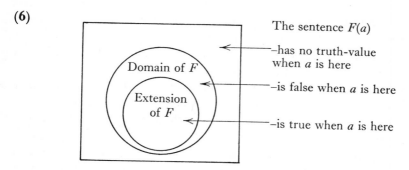

The sentence $F(a)$

—has no truth-value when a is here

—is false when a is here

—is true when a is here

We could thus regard the condition that the subject of a predicate exists as a restriction on the domain of the predicate. Notice that there are certain predicates which do not presuppose existence (at least not in the physical sense) (e.g. (7)).

(7)   Superman is popular

However, these problems are too complex to be satisfactorily treated here.

On p. 74, we gave rules for the truth-conditions of atomic sentences in a normal (presuppositionless) predicate logic. The rules we obtain in a logic with truth-valueless sentences are not very different: the most important thing is that we get three cases instead of two. We can write as follows (for sentences with one-place predicates).

(8)   A sentence of the form $P(t)$ in an arbitrary interpretation

IS TRUE   iff the object that is assigned to the individual term is in the extension of the predicate

IS FALSE   iff the object that is assigned to the individual term is in the domain but not in the extension of the predicate

HAS NO TRUTH-VALUE   otherwise, i.e. iff the object assigned to the individual term is not in the domain of the predicate

The concept of a **definite description** is closely connected with the problem of presuppositions. A definite description is an expression which picks out a certain individual object by describing it as 'the object which has such and such a property'. In the language of ordinary predicate logic, there are no definite descriptions, but it can be extended by introducing a logical constant called the **iota-operator** (ι, the Greek letter iota). Using this operator, we can write e.g. 'the x which is such that it has the property F' as $\iota x(F(x))$. This expression is then used as an individual constant (in the same way as a, b, c), and it can for instance be an argument of predicates, as in $G(\iota x(F(x))$, which is read 'the x which has the property F has the property G' or, in shorter form, 'the F is G'. The iota-operator looks a little like a quantifier, but it is important to understand the difference. A quantifier is put in front of an open sentence and makes it into a sentence, but the iota-operator makes an open sentence into a term (an individual constant). (For a third kind of operator, see the discussion below about the abstraction operator.)

There are certain conditions for using an expression such as $\iota x(F(x))$: there must be an x with the property F and there must not be more than one x with this property. What is the nature of these conditions? Are they truth-conditions or not? One alternative – which was advocated by the British philosopher P. F. Strawson – is to say that when they are not fulfilled, the sentence (or statement) is neither true nor false: this would be in accordance with the truth-value treatment of presuppositions outlined above. However, there is also another view, which was formulated by Bertrand Russell, and which favours a strictly two-value logic (where all sentences are either true or false). In this theory, a sentence containing a definite description can be regarded as an abbreviation for a more complex sentence without definite descriptions.

According to Russell, the expression $G(\iota x(F(x)))$ is equivalent to the formula

(9) $\qquad \exists x\,(F(x)\ \&\ G(x)\ \&\ \sim \exists y\,(F(y)\ \&\ x \neq y))$

or in other words

(10) $\qquad$ There is one and only one x which is F and this x is also G

Russell's classic example, *The King of France is bald*, is thus interpreted as

(11) $\qquad$ There is one and only one King of France and he is bald

We can see that (11) is false if there is no King of France or if there is more than one King of France. Whether (11) adequately renders the meaning of *The King of France is bald* is another question.

9.3. **Pragmatic analysis of presuppositions**

An alternative to using truth-values in characterizing what presuppositions are and what goes wrong when a presupposition is not true is provided by the so-called **pragmatic** analysis of presuppositions. This approach holds that one should introduce, besides truth, a concept of **felicity** into the analysis of linguistic meaning. In the same way that truth relates sentences to situations of which they are true, **felicity** relates sentences to contexts (or situations) in which they are **appropriate** or **felicitous**. The **felicity-conditions** of a sentence are those conditions that must be met by a context in order for a sentence to be felicitous in that context. There are two ways of construing the relation between felicity and truth. Either one can view truth as a type of felicity, or one can more narrowly view truth and felicity as two independent dimensions. If truth and felicity are viewed as two separate dimensions there seem to be certain factors in a speech situation which would seem to affect felicity, but which do not affect truth, and vice versa.

For example, if in a country like France, where there is a distinction between a formal and an informal second-person pronoun (*vous* and *tu*), one says, after having invited some older person one does not know, *Tu es invité* 'You are invited', this would be inappropriate but true. Likewise there are other cases where a sentence could be both infelicitous and false, or conversely felicitous and true or false.[2]

Some of the most important felicity-conditions are created by communicative norms of the type we mentioned above in connection with

---

[2] For an account of the concept of felicity, see Austin (1962).

our discussion of disjunction.[3] Important such norms are: **the norm of competence** and **the norm of relevance or point**. The norm of competence states that a speaker should be sincere and have some foundation for what he says. In the case of statements, this means that he should believe that what he is stating is true and that he should have some evidence to back it up with. Similar implications apply to other types of locution.

The norm of relevance or point says that every linguistic utterance should have some point, i.e. be relevant to some purpose at hand. For statements the point is usually to convey new information.

(1)   Mr Jones is sober today

If we study (1), we see that we are so used to assuming that a statement conveys new information that we implicitly assume a background against which new information would be conveyed, in this case that Jones usually is drunk. If Jones usually is sober we feel that the utterance is pointless, even if it is completely true, i.e. infelicitous, and get angry.

Let us now turn to the analysis of definite descriptions again. A pragmatic analysis of definite descriptions would have something of the following look. First we try to determine what the point of using definite descriptions usually is. In most cases, they are used in order to REFER, which in its turn is done in order to state something about what we are referring to. From other facts about human communication which have to do with the human capacity for transferring and receiving information, we know that this is achieved most effectively if new information can be anchored in old information. The referring part of a statement provides such an anchorage or background against which new information can be asserted. It is thus important that what is referred to is common ground for speaker and listener, i.e. that they both – or at least the speaker – be able to pick out or identify that which is being referred to. This is precisely one of the things we meant to imply when we said that the norm of competence requires the speaker to have some foundation or evidence for that which he asserts. So when a speaker in stating something uses a definite description to indicate what he is speaking about he should be able to identify whatever he is referring to. In order for him to be successful in such an identification, it usually follows (depending on the type of predicate; see above) of course that the

[3] See Grice (1975).

object or phenomenon to which he is referring exists. In other words, whatever is referred to must exist.

The pragmatic analysis in a similar way tries to analyse other types of presupposition like the factive or categorial types of presupposition. On the basis of such analyses it is then claimed that presuppositions are among the factors that determine the felicity of a sentence rather than determining whether a sentence should have a truth-value or not. Thus

(2)   Fafnir's car is red

will be treated as infelicitous and false in the case where Fafnir has no car. False, since our world is not such that (2) could be true in it. 'Not true' can therefore continue to be regarded as a synonym of 'false'. This of course makes the pragmatic analysis similar to Russell's in that a two-valued logic is preserved, but different from his analysis in that the job was done by either a third truth-value or alternatively a **truth-value gap** in our first analysis now is done by felicity-conditions based on a broader analysis of linguistic communication.

It should be said finally that the question of whether a felicity- or a truth-value analysis of presupposition is best is far from solved, and that there are many cases where it is highly unclear whether one should regard a certain condition as a truth-condition or as a felicity-condition in the narrow sense. It is even unclear if these alternatives exclude each other. However, by exhibiting both of these alternatives to the analysis of presupposition (there are others not mentioned here) we have wanted to indicate some of the options available in a formal analysis of linguistic meaning.

9.4.   The abstraction- or lambda-operator

In the chapter on set theory, we mentioned the notation used to define sets by description, $\{x \mid \ldots\}$, read as 'the set of all x such that ...'

There is an alternative way of writing such formulas, by using the so-called **abstraction-** or **lambda**-operator. For instance, to denote 'the set of all x such that $F(x)$', we may write $(\lambda x)(F(x))$ (λ is the Greek letter lambda.[4] If we like, we can regard this operator as an alternative

---

[4] The lambda-operator was introduced by the logician Alonzo Church in his so-called lambda calculus and has been very important in the development of computer language. In Church's system, the lambda-operator was used to represent the function from the objects that can be

to the iota-operator but without its presuppositions (of existence and uniqueness) and referring to a set rather than to an individual. If the iota-operator corresponds to the definite article in the singular, the lambda-operator might be said to correspond to the definite article in the plural. (If this is taken as a linguistic theory, it is rather counter-intuitive, since it assumes that the definite articles in the singular and plural are fundamentally different things.)

There is perhaps another way of interpreting the lambda-operator. We may think of the lambda-expression as denoting a property, for instance, in the case mentioned above, 'the property of being F'. It may then be used either as a term in second-order logic which refers to a property, or, in first-order logic, as a derived predicate expression which can be used to form a sentence together with an individual term. We might write e.g.

(1) $((\lambda x)(F(x)))(a)$

to mean 'a has the property of being F'. This, of course, would be equivalent to $F(a)$. Generally, expressions with lambda-operators in predicate position can be reduced to expressions without them, so that there would not appear to be any prima facie reason why they should be used at all. There is, however, at least one area where they are useful, and that is in modal logic.

In section 7.4, we discussed various ambiguities that can be repre-ented in modal logic as depending on scope differences. We mentioned then that this was somewhat complicated when the ambiguities involved definite descriptions. Now we have introduced the formal means which are necessary to formalize these cases. The example we gave was as follows.

(2)   John believes that the man who robbed him was red-haired

Let us first consider the simple sentence (3).

(3)   The man who robbed John was red-haired

We represent 'x robs y' as $R(x, y)$ and 'x is red-haired' as $H(x)$. With the help of the iota-operator discussed in section 9.3, we get the following.

(4) $H(\iota x(R(x, j)))$

(2) will now be formalized as follows.

values of the variable bound by the operator to the propositions expressed by the sentences obtained if one fixes the reference of the variable to these objects.

(5) $B_j H(\iota x(R(x, j)))$

However, to be able to represent the *de re* reading of (2), we would need a formalization where the description $\iota x(R(x, j))$ appears outside the scope of the operator B_j. Here, the lambda-operator can help us. What we want is something which can be paraphrased as (6).

(6)   The man who robbed John is such (or has the property) that John believes he is red-haired

We thus need a predicate with the meaning 'to be an x such that John believes that he is red-haired'. This can be written $(\lambda x)(B_j(H(x)))$. We can now predicate (7) of the man who robbed John.

(7) $((\lambda x)(B_j(H(x))))(\iota y(R(y, j)))$

  (We use y instead of x as a variable in the iota-expression in order to show more clearly that it is not bound by the lambda-operator)

This somewhat forbidding-looking formula now represents the *de re* reading of (2). The *de dicto* reading was rendered by the simpler formula (5).

10

Logic for linguists?

10.1. General

In this final chapter, we shall discuss the relations between logic and linguistics and the extent to which logic provides useful insights for the study of natural language. It goes without saying that these problems are more controversial than those we have discussed in previous chapters.

Suppose that we want to know what logic can tell us about meaning and the semantic structure of natural language. The following are some of the questions that then arise.

(1) What concept of 'meaning' is found in logic? Is this concept useful for linguistic purposes?

(2) In what way can the formal languages of logic be used when we try to describe the meanings of expressions in natural language?

(3) Are the languages of logic sufficiently rich to serve as models for the semantics of natural languages? If the answer is no, is there any way to remedy the deficiencies?

Why these questions are asked may not be immediately obvious to the reader, but part of the understanding of the relations between logic and language consists in fact in grasping why they must be asked.

10.2. The concept of meaning

Let us begin with the first question. We should distinguish the following two fundamental problems of semantics.

(a) What is meaning in general?

(b) What are the meanings of particular expressions in a language?

Both these questions are notoriously difficult to answer. One of the main reasons for this is that, unlike other branches of science, semantics does not describe things in the world directly but rather describes the tools that are usually used to describe things in the world. The problem is that we must either use these tools to describe themselves – i.e. use ordinary language when describing ordinary language – or find some entirely new tools – i.e. invent some new language to use as a meta-language. In the second case, however, we must use ordinary language as a starting-point when explaining the language we are inventing.

Another reason for the elusiveness of meaning is that the meanings of expressions in languages are entities of an abstract, 'intangible' character. This fact makes it of course much more difficult to verify and falsify semantic hypotheses, which has led people – in particular in formal logic – to try to do away with meanings altogether or to re-interpret the concept of meaning so as to avoid as far as possible the postulation of any theoretical constructs. In fact, when modern systems of formal logic were first developed, they were thought of by many of their students as a purely SYNTACTIC study. Logical consequence was regarded as a relation between expressions in the formal language, and the rules of deduction that permitted one to conclude something from something else were thought of as independent of the interpretation of the expressions, taking into account only their form.

It was only later that logical or model-theoretical semantics was developed. Model-theoretical semantics tries to explain meanings purely in terms of set-theoretical notions such as sets and functions. Let us now look a bit closer at this concept of meaning.

The meanings of expressions tie them to the world or to entities in the world in sometimes complicated fashions. For instance, a predicate is related to a set of entities in the world, more specifically to the set of entities that the predicate can truly be predicated of. If we want to avoid postulating abstract, intangible entities in our semantics, one way is to say that the only interesting thing about predicate is this set – the EXTENSION of the predicate. This was also what was done when people first tried to give a formal semantics for predicate logic – they supposed that one could avoid talking about the meanings of expressions if one chose instead to talk about their extensions. However, as we saw in the chapter on intensional logic, this means that we have to treat non-synonymous expressions – e.g. *Orestes* and *the brother of Electra* – as equivalent if they happen to have the same extension. The way out suggested in that chapter was to postulate something called INTENSIONS. We shall now discuss the problem of whether intensions as they are understood in intensional logic can be identified with the meanings of linguistic expressions. To start with, let us look at the relations between intensions and extensions.

We have already seen that knowing the extension of an expression does not entail knowing its intension, since non-synonymous expressions may have the same extension. What about the converse question: does one know the extension of an expression if one knows its intension? Clearly not: I may very well understand what the expression *be intelligent* means and yet not know exactly who is intelligent and who is not. In other words, to know the extension of an expression I need to know two things: the intension of the expression and what the world is actually like. In fact, we can take this as a definition of the extension of an expression: that which we know provided that we know the intension of the expression and what the world is like. This, incidentally, throws light on the conception of truth-values as the extensions of sentences, which has puzzled many people: if you know what a sentence means and you know what the world is like, you can tell whether the sentence is true or false.

What we have done now is to characterize extensions in terms of intensions. We can also do it the other way round and ask how we can explain the concept of an intension in terms of extension. From this point of view, which was the one adopted in chapter 8, an intension might be said to be an **extension-determining** principle: a rule by which we look at the world and find out the extension of the expression.

The question is now how to specify these principles. Here we are back to the problem discussed above: how can we describe the meanings of expressions belonging to a certain language without making crucial use of this language itself? Intensional logic, as we have seen, claims to have a way out: instead of talking about principles that determine extensions by looking at the world, we can talk about **functions from possible worlds to extensions**. Is there any difference? In the chapter on set theory, we said that a function is a way to assign some entity to each member in a set (the domain of the function). There are several different ways of understanding such a definition, and the answer to the question depends on the interpretation we choose. One possibility is to identify the function with a rule for assigning values to its arguments: in this version, extension-determining functions and extension-determining principles are the same thing. Another, which is favoured by logicians, is to identify the function with the set of all ordered pairs where the first member is an argument of the function and the second is the value of the function for that argument. The reason why the latter alternative is usually preferred is that it reduces functions to a kind of entity that we already have in set theory: sets and ordered pairs. However, if we take the view that intensions of expressions are actually sets of ordered pairs, we will have problems, at least if we identify intensions and meanings and want our semantic theory to have some psychological reality. Since there is – presumably – an infinite number of possible worlds, we would have to claim that when a person learns the meaning of an expression, he learns infinite sets of ordered pairs. We are thus faced with the following dilemma: either we return to the more intuitive way of looking at intensions but give up the chance to make our concepts reducible to set theory, or we keep the definition of intensions as sets of ordered pairs and give up the hope of psychological reality.

There are also other difficulties attendant on the identification of intensions with functions from possible worlds to extensions. We mentioned earlier the case of expressions which have the same extensions but different intensions. It would seem that we do not get the same difficulty in model-theoretical semantics: for instance, there are presumably logically possible worlds where Walter Scott did not write *Waverley*, so the functions which are the intensions of the two NPs *Walter Scott* and *the author of 'Waverley'* would not have the same value for all arguments and would thus be different. Suppose, however, that we choose another example instead, which is taken from Frege. According to Frege, the mathematical expressions '3 + 1' and '2 + 2' would have the same extension ('*Bedeutung*'), viz. the number 4, but different intensions ('*Sinn*'). The idea behind this is that '3 + 1' and '2 + 2' represent two different ways or **procedures** for obtaining the same result. However, if '2 + 2 = 3 + 1' is a logical truth, as true sentences in arithmetic are usually considered to be, the values of '2 + 2' and '3 + 1' are the same, viz. the number 4, in all logically possible worlds. In other words, the expressions '3 + 1' and '2 + 2' correspond to identical functions from possible worlds to numbers, and thus ought to have the same intensions. Generally, if we understand intensions as functions from possible worlds to entities, logically equivalent expressions come out as having the same intensions. The Fregean idea that the intension is the way the extension is obtained clearly gets lost here.

The same problem crops up in particular in connection with the interpretation of propositional attitudes. Suppose we claim the following.

(a) Propositional attitudes are relations between persons and propositions.

(b) Propositions are functions from possible worlds to truth values.

As we said, any two logically equivalent expressions correspond to the same function from possible worlds, so any two logically equivalent sentences will in fact correspond to the same proposition. For instance, all logical truths express the same proposition: the **necessary** proposition which is true in all worlds (the function that has the value 'true' for all possible worlds). But consider a propositional attitude such as belief. Clearly one can believe one logical truth without believing another. For instance, suppose one of my friends in the Logic Department claims to have proved two theorems. He happens to be right, but I have not seen the proofs yet and cannot make any judgement about them. So I choose to believe his first theorem and disbelieve the second. But if both theorems are logical truths and express the same proposition, this ought not to be possible. (Hintikka's treatment of the concept of belief, which was mentioned on p. 113, entails that if one believes p, one also believes all the consequences of p, and thus meets with the same difficulties.)

There are various proposals for getting out of the dilemma related here. One that deserves mentioning is the one put forward by Carnap: he suggests that linguistic synonymy should not be defined as sameness of intensions in the model-theoretical sense but rather as something stronger which involves what he calls **intensional isomorphism**. Roughly, two expressions are intensionally isomorphic if they are built up by constituent expressions which have the same intensions and which are, in their turn, built up by constituents with the same intensions. We see that this comes closer to what Frege meant by '*Sinn*'. In fact, we have already introduced a concept in terms of which intensional isomorphism can be defined. In the discussion of intensional logic and categorial grammar, we said that a sentence has a syntactic and a semantic derivation, both of which can be represented in tree form. The semantic derivation showed us how the interpretation of the whole expression was obtained from the interpretations of its parts. Thus, two expressions would be intensionally isomorphic if they had the same semantic derivation, as this concept was defined above.

We should also discuss here the identification of 'meaning' and 'truth-conditions' (for sentences). There are several kinds of possible objections to this idea, some more and some less serious. Let us dispose of the least serious first. Many linguists react adversely when they first hear statements such as 'the sentence S is true iff...' 'Truth has nothing to do with linguistics', they say; 'it is not the linguist's job to tell what sentences are true and what are false.' This objection is founded on a confusion of two quite different things: the truth-value of a sentence and the truth-conditions of a sentence. Certainly it is not a linguist's job to specify what sentences in a language are actually true; but to specify the conditions under which they are true is quite another thing.

Another objection is more serious. Suppose, as was suggested above, we regard the intension of a sentence as a principle by which we assign a truth-value to the sentence in each possible world. As we have already said, we would like our theory to possess some kind of psychological reality, i.e. the elements of the description should in some way correspond to what happens in the language-user's mind. If so, the question arises of whether there is any correlation between what is assigned to a sentence as its interpretation and what we do when we understand an actual utterance of the statement. We would then expect that what we do when we hear a declarative sentence is to look at the world and see whether the sentence is true or false in it. However, what we rather do is to imagine what the world would be like if the sentence were true; and if we think that the speaker is worth believing, we may change our world-view accordingly. So there does not seem to be a very good correspondence between the interpretation of a sentence in truth-conditional semantics and the understanding process. However, the logician has an answer to this. He can refer to a distinction between 'the description of possible languages or grammars as abstract semantic systems whereby symbols are associated with aspects of the world' and 'the description of the psychological and sociological facts whereby a particular one of these abstract systems is one used by a person or population' (the quotations are from Lewis (1972, 170)). Logical semantics would be concerned only with the first of these, and questions about the use of linguistic expressions would not be relevant for it. According to Lewis, 'only confusion comes out of mixing' the two topics in question. One can object, though, that the study of language as a system which associates symbols with aspects of the world is only possible by abstracting from the study of the use of the symbols in the language, and the question for the linguist is whether the abstraction is an empirically interesting one.

The information contained in the semantic rules we have formulated in the preceding chapters tells us how to derive the interpretations of complex expressions from simple expressions in ways that are independent of what particular simple expressions we choose (except for logical constants). In fact, logical semantics tells us little or nothing about how simple expressions should be interpreted. This makes it seem abstract or even pointless to many people, but we should keep in mind that if logical semantics tells us something interesting about how sentences are interpreted, it is mainly about the ways that the interpretations of complex expressions are obtained from the interpretations of simple expressions or, if we like, of the contribution of STRUCTURE to meaning. We should not expect logical semantics to tell us exactly in which situations a sentence like *It is raining* is true: it might, however, tell us something about the relations between the respective situations when this sentence and its negation, *It is not raining*, are true.

10.3. **The role of formal languages in analysing natural language**

Let us now discuss the second question we formulated in the beginning of this chapter: in what way can the formal languages of logic be used when we try to describe the meanings of expressions in natural languages?

First, it may be appropriate to consider the motives for constructing formal languages in the first place. As we have had occasion to emphasize before, the logician's main object of study is not natural language per se but rather logical arguments. The structure of linguistic expressions is of interest to the logician only to the extent that knowledge of this structure helps him to formulate rules for making correct deductions. But, on the other hand, since almost all aspects of the semantic structure of a sentence can play a role in some form of argument, almost everything in the semantics of natural language is of potential interest to the logician. For this reason, it should not be of any great importance whether one is primarily interested in logical arguments or in expressions in the language. There are other factors, however, which complicate the situation. In the beginning, logicians studied sentences in natural languages and their logical relations. It was soon found that these sentences had troublesome properties such as vagueness, ambiguity, structural unperspicuity and contextually dependent meaning.

This led in due course to attempts to construct ways of representing meanings that would not have these regrettable drawbacks.

The 'formal languages' described in the preceding chapters have been constructed with such an aim. However, it is possible to find a certain confusion in works in logic as to the exact relations between logical formulas and the sentences in natural languages that they are supposed to 'formalize' or 'translate'. For the linguist who studies logic in the hope of learning something about the nature of meaning, the question what these relations are is of course of prime importance, although the answer may not be very easy to find.

In chapter 3 we discussed the concept of logical form. We found, for instance, that the two arguments (5) and (6) on p. 17 'had the same logical form' where 'logical form' was said to be those common properties of the arguments that made them valid. In section 3.2 we said that the logical form of arguments and sentences depends on the presence of certain 'logical words or particles'. Actually, such an account of logical form, which is that found in most textbooks of logic, meets with several kinds of difficulty when applied to natural language. To start with, it is not clear what words should be regarded as 'logical'. In fact, as was pointed out in section 3.7, 'The depth of logical analysis', different systems of logic (propositional logic, predicate logic, modal logic etc.) take account of quite different aspects of the structure of sentences. Each system has its own set of 'logical words and particles' or, to use a technical term, **logical constants**. These logical constants are expressions for those concepts which the particular system focuses on. It is certainly possible to treat a large number of words and morphemes in natural languages as logical constants that have not yet been so treated in any existing formal system. From this point of view, one could argue that one should not talk about 'the logical form of a sentence' but only about 'the logical form of a sentence on the propositional logic level', 'the logical form of a sentence on the predicate logic level' etc. In other words, 'logical form' would be relative to the logical system we are working with.

Furthermore, the traditional account of logical form is misleading, since it centres on the presence or absence of words and morphemes in a sentence and disregards other questions of structure. To take a simple example, the presence of a word of negation (*not*) in a sentence does not tell us anything definite about the conclusions we may draw from the sentence and consequently about its logical form, in so far as we do not know if the negation operates on the whole sentence or not (cf. p. 31). But as soon as we acknowledge that structure is important for logical form, the question arises: what kind of structure? The emphasis on formal criteria in logic makes one look for structural properties of the sentence of a kind that can be determined just by looking at it, i.e. overtly manifested structural properties. But the trouble is that what we want to know about the structure of the sentence is not always there 'on the surface'. This is shown among other things by the existence of structurally ambiguous sentences in natural language. For instance, as was pointed out on p. 68, an English sentence which contains several quantifiers may correspond to more than one formula in predicate logic, depending on the scope of the quantifiers. Thus, the logical structure of a sentence may be **covert**. Knowledge of this fact is implicit in many jokes and riddles that exploit e.g. the existence of sentences which look the same but are in fact quite different. Cf. the following quotation from Lewis Carroll: '"I see nobody on the road", said Alice. "I only wish *I* had such eyes", the King remarked in a fretful tone. "To be able to see Nobody! And at that distance too! Why, it's as much as *I* can do to see real people, by this light"..."Who did you pass on the road?" the King went on, holding out his hand to the Messenger..."Nobody", said the Messenger. "Quite right", said the King: "this young lady saw him too. So of course Nobody walks slower than you." "I do my best", the Messenger said in a sullen tone. "I'm sure nobody walks much faster than I do!" "He can't do that", said the King, "or else he'd have been here first..."'

Obviously, the mistake here is to treat sentences like *I saw nobody on the road* and *I saw John on the road* as having the same logical structure or form. We have seen that the logical form of a sentence may be covert. Some logicians have claimed that this is the case much more often than is usually thought. Thus, Bertrand Russell claimed that sentences containing definite descriptions have quite another logical form than the one their overt grammatical structure would suggest (see p. 153).

The implication of the existence of covert logical properties in natural-language sentences is that if we want to formulate deduction rules that are to look exclusively at the form of sentences, we cannot formulate these deduction rules for sentences in natural language but must construct a 'formal language' into which the natural-language sentences are translated. Indeed, this is one of the main motivations for constructing formal languages.

The idea of covert structures is also prominent in transformational grammar, where the distinction between **surface** and **deep structure** plays an important role. In Chomsky's 'standard theory' (Chomsky (1965)), the deep structure of a sentence is the underlying syntactic structure which determines the semantic interpretation of the sentence. Later, the so-called 'generative semanticists' (Lakoff, McCawley, Postal, Ross) claimed that the deep structure of the sentence was identical to its 'semantic representation'. Still later, the term 'logical form' was used to refer to this level of description. Accordingly, the 'semantic representations' postulated by generative semanticists looked very much like formulas in predicate logic.

This idea could be discussed at length, but we shall restrict ourselves to pointing out a few things that should be kept in mind, without claiming that generative semanticists have not been aware of them. First, we should notice the difference between a 'semantic representation' and a 'semantic interpretation'. A semantic representation is a way of displaying what a sentence means; it is not the meaning itself. Most frequently, a semantic representation is something which is in effect an expression in another language. In particular, if formulas in predicate logic are regarded as the semantic representations of expressions in English or some other human language, it is clear that these representations are also expressions in a language – the language of predicate logic – which has its own syntax and semantics. In other words, the rules that relate semantic representations and surface syntactic forms must be complemented with rules that interpret the semantic representations – for instance, with the rules on pp. 83–4.

Since one of the main properties that are thought to distinguish semantic representations and surface syntactic structures is that the former are unambiguous, we could say that what we do when providing semantic representations irrespective of what they look like is to construct a **disambiguated language**, which cannot be the final result of the process of providing semantic interpretations for sentences, but must be an intermediate stage only. We can represent this process as follows.

$$\text{Syntactic structures} \longleftrightarrow \begin{array}{c}\text{Expressions}\\ \text{in the dis-}\\ \text{ambiguated}\\ \text{language}\end{array} \longleftrightarrow \begin{array}{c}\text{Semantic}\\ \text{interpretation}\end{array}$$

One should then ask oneself why the intermediate stage should be there at all and why we could not instead have the following, simpler model.

Syntactic   Semantic
structures ⟷   interpretations

Notice that there is nothing in principle that would prevent the rules of semantic interpretation from having several outputs for one sentence.

There are of course several possible arguments for the existence of an intermediate stage. One argument has already been mentioned: the desire to be able to construct formal deduction rules. In our opinion, the most reasonable way of defending the use of a disambiguated language is to say that we need some way of referring to the semantic interpretations in any case, so we have to construct a disambiguated language to do that. This view is acceptable so long as one keeps in mind that the 'semantic representations' or expressions in the disambiguated language are only an auxiliary device and have no independent status in themselves. What we should beware of is mixing up the syntactic categories of the disambiguated language, e.g. 'sentence' and 'predicate', with the categories of semantic interpretation, e.g. 'proposition' and 'property'.

As was mentioned on p. 146, the method of using a disambiguated language as an intermediate stage in the process of assigning semantic interpretations to sentences in English was employed by Richard Montague in some of his papers (Montague (1974, ch. 7)). In his work, the auxiliary character of the disambiguated language is perfectly clear.

Notice that what has been said above is in fact independent of the nature of semantic interpretations: whether they should be thought of as being representable as 'trees' of the type illustrated above or as being radically different.

10.4. The limitations of classical logic

Finally, we must try to answer the last question that we formulated at the beginning of this chapter: are the languages of logic sufficiently rich to serve as models for the semantics of natural languages? If the answer is no, is there any way to remedy the deficiencies?

Since first-order predicate logic is often regarded as a kind of classical logical system, we could start by seeing if there are distinctions in natural language that have no counterparts in predicate logic and ask ourselves whether these distinctions have semantic relevance.

We have already seen that only a few of the 'sentential connectives' (coordinating conjunctions) and 'quantifiers' (numerals, quantifying adjectives etc.) of natural language can be directly translated into predicate logic. We also mentioned that the usual formalizations of sentences such as *All girls are beautiful* are rather dubious from various points of view.

The distinctions between major lexical classes (nouns, adjectives and verbs) of natural language are not upheld in predicate logic. Whereas proper nouns are translated as individual terms, common nouns, adjectives and verbs are all lumped together as predicates. Some logicians, e.g. Reichenbach, and the adherents of generative semantics have claimed this to be a virtue of predicate logic and a deficiency of traditional grammar. But clearly, the lexical classes are not semantically irrelevant: how the differences between them should be captured is, however, an open question.

In the same way, the sub-classes of common nouns (countable nouns and mass nouns) have no counterparts in predicate logic. In general, sentences with mass nouns are hard to formalize in the language of predicate logic. The reader might try out for himself a sentence such as (1).

(1)   Gold is scarce these days but I bought some today (It should be conceded, however, that there are a number of other reasons why (1) is hard to formalize)

Some parts of speech do not seem to have any counterparts at all in logic, e.g. subordinating conjunctions, prepositions (perhaps another kind of predicate) and various types of adverb (but cf. p. 148 above).

We have already discussed the relations between the definite article of e.g. English and the iota-operator of (extended) predicate logic.

Sentences such as the following, some of which are called 'generic' in linguistic descriptions, cannot be distinguished within predicate logic.

(2)   (a)   Dogs bark
        (b)   The dog barks (where *the dog* is taken to refer to the species)
        (c)   All dogs bark
        (d)   The dogs bark
        (e)   All the dogs bark
        (f)   A dog barks

Presumably, they would all be represented as (3).

(3) $\qquad \forall x\, (D(x) \to B(z))$

Sentences (d) and (e) refer to some definite set of dogs which is given in the speech situation, whereas the others are understood as general statements about the species 'dog'. A theory which accounts for this will have to include a mechanism which allows the universe of discourse to change during the course of a conversation and some way of expressing 'general laws'. The latter might be arrived at with the help of modal logic: we would want to say that e.g. (a) is not only about the actual dogs that happen to exist in our world but about all dogs that exist in the possible worlds where the laws of nature are the same as in our world.

We would also need a mechanism to distinguish the sentences with *all* from the sentences without this word. In natural language, we may take general statements that are not necessarily falsified by a single counter-example, as the corresponding expressions with the universal quantifier in predicate logic would be. For instance, we would not say that we have shown that (a) is false if we have found one dog which does not bark.

Perhaps the most conspicuous limitation of predicate logic is that it accounts only for declarative sentences. Imperative and interrogative sentences fall entirely outside the system. The reason is that these kinds of sentence have quite different functions in speech acts: they are not normally used to convey information about the world. Attempts have been made, however, to construct 'imperative logics' and 'question logics'. Opinions are divided as to the correct treatment of these sentence types. Some logicians (and linguists) think that it is possible to treat them as special types of declarative sentences: this would make it possible to assign truth-conditions to them. One fairly widespread theory to this effect is the **performative hypothesis**: according to this theory, all sentences would have underlying structures in which the highest clause is a statement by the speaker of what he does in the speech act he is performing: for instance, an imperative sentence would have the underlying structure *I order you that S*. There are also other hypotheses.

But the meanings of declarative sentences also – as 'meaning' is usually understood – include aspects that cannot very easily be interpreted as truth-conditional. For instance, it is hard to think of a situation where one of the sentences in (4) would be true and the other false, but still they clearly differ in meaning.

(4) (a) The glass was half empty
(b) The glass was half full

Opinions are divided also as to what aspects of the semantics of declarative sentences can be regarded as truth-conditional, as we saw in the section on presuppositions. We could also mention sentences expressing value-judgements, e.g. (5)–(6), which, according to some theories of moral philosophy, are not true or false at all.

(5) It is immoral to have sexual intercourse without being married
(6) Milton was a great poet

Thus, although the limitations of predicate logic are clear, many logicians and linguists are at present working at extending predicate logic or constructing alternative systems that are better suited to serving as models for the semantics of natural language. It is, of course, an open question to what extent they will succeed and whether the fundamental ideas of logical semantics are adequate for handling the problems of natural language. Whatever the outcome, we think there are several reasons why semantically oriented linguists need to study logic. First, knowledge of the fundamental concepts of logic is necessary in order to understand almost any serious present-day work in linguistic semantics. Second, logicians have tried to answer a number of questions which are central to any kind of semantic theory, such as: What kind of object or entity are the meanings of linguistic expressions? How are linguistic expressions tied to things in the outside world? How is it possible to interpret an unlimited number of complex expressions when one has at one's disposal the knowledge of the interpretations of a limited number of simple expressions? What are the relations between language and reasoning? How can we describe the meanings of an infinite set of sentences with a finite set of semantic rules?

The answers they have given may not be the final ones, but they are in some cases the only ones that exist so far. Third, the formal systems constructed by logicians have the great advantage of being EXPLICIT. The development of generative grammar has made linguists understand that an explicit model – even one which is wrong – may help us to gain insight into problems by making clear exactly what we know and what we do not know. We obtain new insights into human language by studying the very limitations of the logical model of it.

References

Ajdukiewicz, K. 1935. 'Die syntaktische Konnexität', *Studia Philosophica* (Warsaw), 1, 1–28.

Anderson, J. and Johnstone, H. 1962. *Natural Deduction*, Belmont, Calif.: Wadsworth.

Austin, J. L. 1962. *How to Do Things with Words*, Oxford: University Press.

Bar-Hillel, Y. 1970. *Aspects of Language*, Jerusalem: Magnes Press.

Carnap, R. 1947. *Meaning and Necessity*, Chicago: University of Chicago Press.

1958. *Introduction to Symbolic Logic and Its Applications*, New York: Dover.

Chomsky, N. 1957. *Syntactic Structures*, The Hague: Mouton.

1965. *Aspects of a Theory of Syntax*. Cambridge, Mass.: M.I.T. Press.

Cooper, D. 1974. *Presupposition*, The Hague: Mouton.

Cooper, R. and Parsons, T. 1976. 'Montague grammar, generative semantics and interpretative semantics', in B. Partee (ed.), *Montague Grammar*, New York: Academic Press, pp. 311–62.

Cresswell, M. 1973. *Logics and Languages*, London: Methuen.

Davidson, D. and Harman, G. (eds.) 1972. *Semantics of Natural Language*, Dordrecht: Reidel.

Davies, P. 1973. *Modern Theories of Language*, Englewood Cliffs, N.J.: Prentice-Hall.

Fillmore, C. J. and Langendoen, D. T. (eds.) 1971. *Studies in Linguistic Semantics*, New York and London: Macmillan.

Fodor, J. and Katz, J. J. 1963. 'The structure of a semantic theory', *Language* 39, 170–210.

van Fraassen, B. C. 1971. *Formal Semantics and Logic*, New York and London: Macmillan.

Frege, G. 1952. 'Ueber Sinn und Bedeutung', in P. Geach and M. Black (trs. and eds.), *Translations from the Philosophical Writings of Gottlob Frege*, Oxford: Blackwell, pp. 56–78.

Geach, P. 1972. 'A program for syntax', in Davidson and Harman (eds.) 1972, pp. 483–97.

Grice, H. P. 1975. 'Logic and conversation' in P. Cole and J. Morgan (eds.), *Syntax and Semantics*, III, New York: Academic Press, pp. 41–58.

Halmos, P. R. 1960. *Naive Set Theory*, Princeton, N.J.; Van Nostrand.

Hintikka, J. 1962. *Knowledge and Belief: An Introduction to the Logic of the Two Notions*, Ithaca, N.Y. and London: Cornell University Press.

1969. *Models for Modalities*, Dordrecht: Reidel.

Hughes, G. E. & Cresswell, M. J. 1968. *An Introduction to Modal Logic*, London: Methuen.

Husserl, E. 1962. *Ideas*, London: Collier.

Kalish, D. and Montague, R. 1964. *Logic*, New York: Harcourt, Brace and World.

Kaplan, D. 1963. 'Foundations of intensional logic', unpublished Ph.D. thesis, University of California at Los Angeles.

Katz, J. J. 1972. *Semantic Theory*, New York: Harper and Row.

Katz, J. J. and Postal, P. 1964. *An Integrated Theory of Linguistic Descriptions*, Cambridge, Mass.: M.I.T. Press.

Kneale, M. and Kneale, W. 1962. *The Development of Logic*, Oxford: University Press.

Kripke, S. 1963. 'Semantical considerations on modal logics', *Acta Philosophica Fennica*, 16, 83–94.

1972. 'Naming and necessity', in Davidson and Harman (eds.), 1972, pp. 253–355.

Lakoff, G. 1970. 'Counterparts, or the problem of reference in transformational grammar', in S. Kuno, *Report No. NSF-24 to the National Science Foundation*, Cambridge, Mass.: Harvard Computational Laboratory, pp. 23–37.

Lambek, J. 1961. 'On the calculus of syntactic types', in R. Jakobson (ed.), *On the Structure of Language and Its Mathematical Aspects*, Providence, R.I.: American Mathematical Society.

Leibniz, G. W. 1952. *Discourse on Metaphysics*, tr. P. Lucas and L. Grint, Manchester: University Press.

Lewis, D. 1968. 'Counterpart theory and quantified modal logic', *Journal of Philosophy*, 65, 113–26.

1972. 'General semantics', in Davidson and Harman (eds.), 1972, pp. 169–218.

1973. *Counterfactuals*, Oxford: Blackwell.

Lipschutz, S. 1964. *Theory and Problems of Set Theory and Related Topics*, New York: Schaum.

Lyons, J. 1968. *Introduction to Theoretical Linguistics*, Cambridge: University Press.

Mates, B. 1965. *Elementary Logic*, Oxford: University Press.

Mendelson, E. 1964. *Introduction to Mathematical Logic*, Princeton, N.J.: Van Nostrand.

Montague, R. 1974. *Formal Philosophy: Selected Papers of Richard Montague*, ed. R. Thomason, New Haven, Conn., and London: Yale University Press.

Olshewsky, T. M. (ed.) 1969. *Problems in the Philosophy of Language*, New York: Holt Rinehart and Winston.

Partee, B. 1975. 'Montague grammar and transformational grammar', *Linguistic Inquiry*, 6: 2, 203–300.

Petöfi, János, S. and Franck, Dorothea (eds.), 1973. *Präsuppositionen in Philosophie und Linguistik/Presuppositions in Philosophy and Linguistics*, Frankfurt: Athenäum.

Post, E. 1936. 'Finite combinatory processes – formulation I', *Journal of Symbolic Logic*, 1, 103–5.

Prior, A. N. 1957. *Time and Modality*, Oxford: University Press.

1967. *Past, Present and Future*, Oxford: University Press.

Prior, A. N. 1968. *Papers on Time and Tense*, Oxford: University Press.

Quine, W. V. O. 1963. *From a Logical Point of View*, New York: Harper.

1964. *Word and Object*, Cambridge, Mass.: M.I.T. Press.

1970. *Philosophy of Logic*, Englewood Cliffs, N.J.: Prentice-Hall.

Reichenbach, H. 1966. *Elements of Symbolic Logic*, New York: Free Press.

Rescher, N. 1968. *Topics in Philosophical Logic*, Dordrecht: Reidel.

Resnik, M. 1970. *Elementary Logic*, New York: McGraw-Hill.

Rosenberg, J. and Travis, C. (eds.) 1971. *Readings in the Philosophy of Language*, Englewood Cliffs, N.J.: Prentice-Hall.

Stalnaker, R. 1968. 'A theory of conditionals', in N. Rescher (ed.), *Studies in Logical Theory*, Oxford: Blackwell, pp. 98–112.

References

Steinberg, D. and Jacobovits, L. A. (eds.) 1971. *Semantics: An Interdisciplinary Reader in Philosophy, Linguistics and Psychology*, Cambridge: University Press.

Stoll, R. R. 1961. *Introduction to Set Theory and Logic*, San Francisco and London: Freeman.

Strawson, P. F. 1967. *Introduction to Logical Theory*, London: Methuen.

Tarski, A. 1965. *Introduction to Logic*, Oxford: University Press.

Thomason, R. 1970. *Symbolic Logic*, London: Macmillan.

Voltaire, 1759. *Candide.*

Answers to exercises

Chapter 2. Set theory

1. (a) $b \in C$; (b) $C \subset D$; (c) $A \cup C$; (d) $\{d, e, g\}$; (e) $d \notin A \cap B$;
(f) $CA \subset B \cup C$

2. (a) the boys whom Mary has kissed
(b) the Danes who are philosophers (the Danish philosophers)

3. {{London}, {Edinburgh}, {Dublin}, {London, Edinburgh}, {London, Dublin}, {Edinburgh, Dublin}, {London, Edinburgh, Dublin}, $\varnothing$}

4. True: (a), (c), (d), (f); false: (b), (e)

5.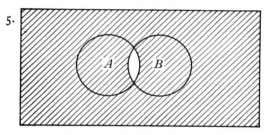

6. True: (a), (b), (d), (e), (g); false: (c), (f)

7. (a) domain: countries; co-domain: cities
(b) domain: men; co-domain: women
(c) domain: schools; co-domain: human beings

Chapter 4. Propositional logic

1. (b), since it cannot be interpreted as $p \,\&\, q$. It is not synonymous with *Oliver is a relative and Richard is a relative.*

2. (a) $p \rightarrow q$; (b) $p \,\&\, q$; (c) $q \rightarrow p$; (d) $(p \lor q) \,\&\, \sim r$;
(e) $\sim (p \lor q) \rightarrow r$; (f) $\sim p \rightarrow q$ or $p \lor q$

3. (a) **f**; (b) **t**; (c) **f**; (d) **t**; (e) **t**; (f) **t**

4. (a), (c), (d), (f), (h)

5. No. A sentence like *John is happy because Mary loves him* can for example be true or false even if both simple sentences are true. The truth-value of *p because q* can therefore not be a function of the truth-value of *p* and *q* alone.

6. (*a*) A*pq*;   (*b*) EN*pq*;   (*c*) EA*pq*K*pq*

7. (*a*) p & $\sim q$;   (*b*) $(((p \equiv q)$ & $r) \vee s) \rightarrow t$;
   (*c*) $(p \rightarrow q) \equiv (\sim q \rightarrow \sim p)$

8. (*a*), (*b*) and (*c*) are all tautologies.

Chapter 5.   Predicate logic

1. (*a*) Burt admires Frank
   (*b*) Burt admires Frank but Frank despises Burt
   (*c*) Someone admires himself
   (*d*) Not everyone despises Frank
   (*e*) Everyone who admires Frank despises himself
   (*f*) It is not the case that there is someone that everyone admires
   (*g*) Everyone who admires someone does not despise that person

2. (*a*) $D(c)$
   (*b*) $L(c)$ & $S(o)$
   (*c*) $\sim \exists x(G(x)$ & $L(x, l))$
   (*d*) $\forall x(S(x) \rightarrow \exists y(B(y)$ & $R(x, y)))$
   (*e*) $\sim \exists x \forall y((S(x)$ & $Q(y)) \rightarrow A(x, y))$
   (*f*) $\forall x(S(x) \rightarrow F(x) \rightarrow \sim \exists x(S(x)$ & $G(x))$
   (*g*) $T(a) \rightarrow C(a)$

3. (*a*) reflexive, symmetric, transitive
   (*b*) reflexive, non-symmetric, transitive
   (*c*) irreflexive, asymmetric, intransitive
   (*d*) non-reflexive, non-symmetric, non-transitive
   (*e*) irreflexive, non-symmetric, non-transitive (in the biological sense of the term, excluding half-brothers)

4. The relation between a person and his fingerprint is probably a one-to-one relation, which means that it is a function.

5. For example: (*a*) 'admire'; (*b*) 'have as result in the test' (each student has a certain result in the test); (*c*) 'be the father of'; (*d*) 'be the husband of' (in a monogamous society)

6. For example: $P(a)$ & $\sim P(a)$
   or $(\forall x(M(x) \rightarrow C(x))$ & $M(b)) \rightarrow \sim C(b)$

7. (*a*) $\exists x(B(x)$ & $S(v, x)$ & $S(k, x))$;
   (*b*) $\exists x(B(x)$ & $S(v, x))$ & $\exists y(B(y)$ & $S(k, x))$, where B stands for 'bear' and S for 'saw' and r refers to Roger and k refers to Knut

8. (*a*) $\exists y \forall x H(x, y)$;
   (*b*) $\forall x \exists y H(x, y)$, where H stands for 'hate'

9. For example: 'be bigger than' and 'be smaller than'.

10. A two-place predicate is interpreted as a set of ordered pairs.

11. $\exists x(P(x)\ \&\ E(x))$, where P stands for 'power' and E stands for 'evil'

12. An open sentence is a logical formula with at least one free variable.

13. (a) and (c) are equivalent
    (b) and (f) are equivalent
    (d) and (g) are equivalent

14. (a) G: $\{b, c\}$
    L: $\{\langle a, a\rangle\ \langle c, b\rangle\ \langle b, c\rangle\}$
    (b) G: $\{b, c\}$
    L: $\{\langle a, a\rangle\ \langle c, b\rangle\ \langle b, c\rangle\ \langle a, c\rangle\}$

15. True sentences: (c) and (f)
    False sentences: (a), (b), (d), (e), (g) and (h)
    (To see that h is false is fairly difficult, but if you look at the interpretation, you will see that d likes a and a likes d but d does not like d. And there is nothing that prevents the two variables x and z from referring to the same person, as they do in this example.)

16. (a) $H(a)$
    (b) $\sim H(a)$
    (c) $\sim \forall x L(x, a)$
    (d) $\exists x L(x, c)$
    (e) $\exists x \forall y L(y, x)$

17. The following interpretation makes all the sentences in exercise (1) true.
    A: $\{\langle b, f\rangle\ \langle a, a\rangle\}$
    D: $\{\langle f, b\rangle\ \langle b, b\rangle\}$

Chapter 6. Deduction

1. Existential Generalization.

2. $p \equiv q$ premise
   $(p \rightarrow q)\ \&\ (q \rightarrow p)$ by Equivalence Elimination
   $q \rightarrow p$ by Conjunction Elimination

3. p premise
   $\sim \sim p$ by Double Negation Introduction
   p by Double Negation Elimination

4.┌(a) $(p \to q) \mathbin{\&} (q \to r)$ assumption
 │(b) $p \to q$ from (a) by Conjunction Elimination
 │(c) $q \to r$ from (a) by Conjunction Elimination
 │┌(d) p assumption
 ││(e) q from (b) and (d) by modus ponens
 ││(f) r from (c) and (e) by modus ponens
 │└(g) $p \to r$ from (d)–(f) by Conditionalization
  (h) $((p \to q) \mathbin{\&} (q \to r)) \to (p \to r)$ from (a)–(g) by Conditionalization

5. (a) $p \equiv q$ premise
   (b) q premise
   (c) $(p \to q) \mathbin{\&} (q \to p)$ from (a) by Equivalence Elimination
   (d) $q \to p$ from (c) by Conjunction Elimination
   (e) p from (b) and (d) by modus ponens

6. (a) $S(g) \mathbin{\&} H(g)$ premise
   (b) $\forall x(S(x) \to D(x)) \mathbin{\&} \forall y(H(y) \to M(y))$ premise
   (c) $S(g)$ from (a) by Conjunction Elimination
   (d) $H(g)$ from (a) by Conjunction Elimination
   (e) $\forall x(S(x) \to D(y))$ from (b) by Conjunction Elimination
   (f) $\forall y(H(y) \to M(y))$ from (b) by Conjunction Elimination
   (g) $S(g) \to D(g)$ from (e) by Universal Instantiation
   (h) $H(g) \to M(g)$ from (f) by Universal Instantiation
   (i) $D(g)$ from (c) and (g) by modus ponens
   (j) $M(g)$ from (d) and (h) by modus ponens
   (k) $D(g) \mathbin{\&} M(g)$ from (i) and (j) by Conjunction Introduction

7. (a) $p \mathbin{\&} q$ premise
   (b) p by Conjunction Elimination
   (c) $\sim \sim p$ by Double Negation Introduction

Chapter 7. Modal logic

1. (a) $N\forall x F(x)$; (b) $\forall x(N \exists y(F(x, y)))$

2. $N(p \lor \sim p)$

3. $M\forall x(S(x) \to \exists y(B(y) \mathbin{\&} R(x, y)))$

$\left.\begin{array}{l} M\exists y\forall x \\ \forall x M \exists y \\ \forall x \exists y M \\ \exists y \forall x M \\ \exists y M \forall x \end{array}\right\}$ $S(x) \to B(y) \mathbin{\&} R(x, y)))$

4. The reason that the first argument is fallacious is that *a widow* must be interpreted relative to a temporal reference point; when it occurs in a sentence with a verb in the past tense, this reference-point is naturally taken to be past too. Therefore *a widow* will have different reference-points in the two sentences where it occurs.

Chapter 8.   Intensional logic and categorial grammar

1. Intensional: *worship, look for, imagine*
   Extensional: *eat, drink*

2. (*a*)

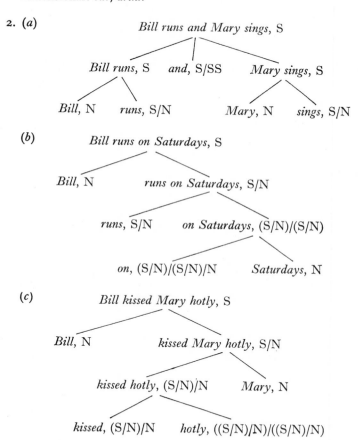

(*b*)

(*c*)

All three sentences can be given different structures. Categorial grammar allows most structures. But the three given here seem most reasonable on semantic grounds. (Thus our structure for (2(*c*)) differs from the one assigned to (5) in the text.)

3. (a)

Bill looks for Mary ⟨ t ⟩

Bill ⟨ s, e ⟩   looks for Mary ⟪ s, e ⟩, t ⟩

looks for ⟨⟨ s, e ⟩, ⟪ s, e ⟩, t ⟩⟩   Mary ⟨ s, e ⟩

(b)

Bill eats the fish ⟨ t ⟩

Bill ⟨ s, e ⟩   eats the fish ⟪ s, e ⟩, t ⟩

eats ⟨⟨ s, e ⟩, ⟪ s, e ⟩, t ⟩⟩ the fish ⟨ s, e ⟩

Can be reduced

(c)

Bill eats the fish quickly ⟨ t ⟩

Bill ⟨ s, e ⟩   eats the fish quickly ⟪ s, e ⟩, t ⟩

eats quickly ⟪ s, e ⟩, ⟪ s, e ⟩, t ⟩⟩   the fish ⟨ s, e ⟩

eats ⟨ s, ⟪ s, e ⟩, ⟪ s, e ⟩, t ⟩⟩⟩ quickly ⟪ s, ⟨ s, ⟪ s, e ⟩, ⟪ s, e ⟩, t ⟩⟩⟩, ⟪ s, e ⟩, ⟪ s, e ⟩, t ⟩⟩⟩

Can be reduced

INDEX

Page numbers in bold type indicate definitions or defining discussions.

abstraction operator 155
accessibility 113
accidental property 119
adjectives 169
Adjukiewicz, Kazimierz 132
adverbs 109, 121, 139, 148, 169
alethic logic 112
all-quantifier **61f**, 115, 169, 170
alternativeness 113
analysis, logical 25f, 58f
analysis tree 136
analytic sentences 23–4
analytic truth and falsehood 23–4
and 4, 25, 30, **32f**
application rules, functional 136
appropriateness 153
argument: of a function 11, 133; of a predicate 60; (= reason) 17, 155
assignment 11
assignment function 84
asymmetric relation 89
atomic sentence 25
Austin, John 153
autonomy of syntax 131
axiom and axiom systems 103

Bar-Hillel, Yehoshua 132
basic categories (of categorial grammar) 133, 135
Bedeutung 126
belief world 114
binding 64
boulomaic logic 112
bound variable 64
box diagram 43

Carnap, Rudolf 126, 128, 162
Carroll, Lewis 166
case 22
categorial grammar 132f
categorial presupposition 150
categorial syntax 135
categories (basic *v.* functional) 133, 135–6

certain 108
certainly 109
characteristic function 13, 137, 144
Chomsky, Noam 167
Church, Alonzo 126, 155
class 3
classical logic, limitations of 168
co-domain 12
collection 3, 6
common nouns 169
communicative norms 153
competence, norm of 154
complement 8
compound sentence 25
concatenation 132
conceivability 112–13
conceptualism 127
conclusion 15
Conditionalization 100
conditions: felicity- 153; truth- **47**, 129, 155, 162
conjunct 32
conjunction 4, 26, 30, **32**; associative 34; commutative 33; coordinating/subordinating 169
Conjunction Elimination 97
Conjunction Introduction 97
connectives 26, **30**, 42, 169
consequence, logical 16, 159
constant: individual 59, 73; logical **27**, 165; predicate 59, 73
constituent structure 42
context: intensional/extensional 139; transparent/opaque 118
context-dependent 121
contingent property 119
contradiction 24, **50f**
converse relation 90
Cooper, Robin 146
coordination 25
co-referring terms 118
counterfactual sentences 39, 120
counterparts 119
covert structure 166

Index

Cresswell, Max 132
cross-world identification 119

de dicto **115**, 118, 157
de re **115**, 118, 157
deduction 96f
deduction rules **98f**, 159; in everyday conversation 104f
deductive logic 16
deductive system 96f
deep structure 146
definite descriptions 149f
deictic expressions 121
deontic logic 111
deontic operators 111
derived (or functional) categories 135
describability 112
description 4; definite 152
desirability 112
diagram: box 43; tree 42
dictionary (or functor) expressions 135
difference 7
direct speech 21
disambiguated language 146, 168
discourse, universe of 5, **62**, 170
disjunct 34
disjunction 30, **34f**; inclusive/exclusive 35
Disjunction Elimination 98
Disjunction Introduction 98
domain: of function 12; of intension 129; of predicate 151
Double Negation Elimination 99
Double Negation Introduction 99

either...or 35–6
Electra paradox 125
elements of a set 3
empty set 4, 6
entailment, logical 16
enumeration 4
epistemic logic 112f
equivalence 30, **40**
equivalence elimination 99
equivalence introduction 99
equivalence relation 90
essential property 119
excluded middle, law of 103
existential generalization 102
existential presupposition 150
existential quantifier 65, 105
explicitness 171
expressions, dictionary 135
extension **4**, 125f, 151, 159
extension-determining principle 160
extensional context 139

extensional predicate 127
extensional set 5
extensional type 136, 144
extensionality principle 4

factive presupposition 150
false 152f
false analytically or in all possible worlds 24
families (of sets) 6
fears 112
felicity 153
first-order predicate logic 58f
form: grammatical 19; logical **17f**, 165, 167
formal language **45**, 164
formation, rules of 44f
formulas, well-formed (wff) 44
free variables 64
Frege, Gottlob 126, 149, 161–2
Fregean principle 130f
function **10–11**, 160; assignment 84; characteristic 12; sentential 63; truth- 27, 37–8, **53**
functional application rules 136
functional categories 133, 135–6
functions from possible worlds to extensions 160
functor 133
functor expression 135
future 123

Geach, Peter 132
general interpreting function 130
generalization, existential 102
generative semantics 167, 169
generic sentences 169
glue (that ties language to the world) 128f
grammatical form 19
group 3

Hintikka, Jaakko 113–14, 162
hopes 112
Husserl, Edmund 132
hyponymy 23
hypotaxis 25

ideal worlds 111
identification, cross-world 119
if 120
if-constructions 110
if...then 37f
implication 30, **37f**
implication, material 38, 110
Implication Elimination 99
Implication Introduction 100

inclusion 6
indexical expressions 121
indices 121
indirect reasoning 53, 105
indirect speech 21
individual concept 137
individual constant 59, 73
individual term 60
individual variable 59
induction, mathematical 46
inductive logic 16
inference: logically valid 15f; (= rule of deduction) 98
information, new/old 154
intension 4, 118, **125f**, 159f; of sentences 136
intensional context 139
intensional grammar 144
intensional isomorphism 162
intensional logic 118, 125f, 159f
intensional predicate 127
intensional type 144
interpretation 73f
interpretation rules, semantic 146
interpreting function, general 130
intersection 6
inter-sentential relations 25
intransitive relation 89
intra-sentential relations 25
iota-operator 152
irreflexive relation 88
isomorphism (between syntax and semantics) 131, 138; intensional 162

Kaplan, David 128
Kripke, Saul 119, 128

labelled parentheses 43
labelling relation 128
labels, node 42–3
Lakoff, George 120, 167
lambda-operator 155
language: disambiguated 167; formal 45, 164; object- 45
law of excluded middle 103
lectons 126
Leibniz, G. W. von 22
Leśniewski, Stanisław 132
Lewis, David 119–20, 163
lexical classes 169
logic: alethic 112; boulomaic 112; deductive/inductive 16; epistemic 112; modal 108f; predicate 58f, 148f; propositional 25f; sentential 25f
logical analysis 25f, 58f
logical connectives 30
logical consequence 159

logical constant 27
logical entailment 16
logical form 17, 18f, 165, 167
logical paradox 125
logical particles 19
logical semantics 72, 159
logical structure 42, 166–7
logical truth 23

McCawley, James 167
main connective 42
many–many relation 91
many–one relation 91
mapping 11, 12, 133
material implication 38, 110
may 112
meaning, concept of 158f
meaning of a linguistic expression 126f
meaning postulate 144
members (of a set) 3
metalanguage 45, 159
metavariables 46
modal logic 108f, 109
modal operators 108–9
modal predicate logic 110
modal propositional logic 110
modal sentential adverbs 139
modal verbs 109
modality 108f; *de dicto/de re* 115
model 73
model–theoretical semantics 73, 159
modus ponens 99
modus tollens 101
Montague, Richard 128, 131, 168
Montague grammar 131; and transformational grammar 146
mood 109
must 112

name 132
naming relation 128
necessary (concept) 109
necessary condition 40
necessary property 119
necessary proposition 162
negation 165; scope of 44
negation connective 30
Negation Introduction 101
node 42
node labels 42–3
non-reflexive relation 89
non-symmetric relation 89
non-transitive relation 89
norms, communicative 153–4
nouns 169

Index

one–many relation 91
object-language 45
opacity 117
opaque context 118
open sentence 59
operation (type of function) 12
operations on sets 6
operators: abstraction 155; deontic 111; iota- 152; lambda- 155; model 109; predicate 148; temporal 121
or 34f
order of quantifiers 67
ordered pair 9
ordered *n*-tuples 10

pair 9
paradox, logical (Electra) 125
parataxis 25
parentheses 42–3
Parsons, Terence 146
particles, logical 19
past tense 123
performative hypothesis 170
phrase-structure rules 46
physical possibility 112
point, norm of 154
Polish notation 57, 109
possibility, logical, physical, practical etc. 112
possible, logically 108–9
possible world 22, 108, 160
possibly 109
Postal, Paul 167
power set 6
pragmatic analysis 152
predicate: constant 59, 73; domain 151; extension 125f, 151; operator 148f; term 60; variable 59
predicate logic: first-order 58f; modal 110; second-order 148f
predication 58
premises 15
prepositions 169
present perfect 123
presuppositions 149f; categorial (or sortal) 150; existential 150; factive 150; pragmatic analysis of 152
Prior, Arthur 121
probability 106
probability theory 109
procedures 161
proper nouns 169
properties 119
proposition 20, 136, 149
propositional attitudes 112, 161
propositional calculus 44

propositional connectives 26, 169
propositional logic 25f, 44f
propositional variables 26

quadruples 10
quantification: restricted 67; vacuous 63
quantifiers 61f, 110, 169; *all-* 62, 115; existential 65, 115; order of 67; scope of 64, 67–8; universal 62
quintuples 10

range of function 12
range of intension 129
range of predicate 62, 67
realism 127
reasoning, indirect 53f, 105
recursive rule 46; general 138
recursivity 131
reductio ad absurdum 53f
reduction (of extensional predicates) 144
reference points 121
reflexive relation 88f
reflexivity **88**, 113
regimentation (of natural language) 146
Reichenbach, Hans 148, 169
relation 10, **88f**
relations, formal properties of 88f
relations and functions 9
relations between sets 5
relative clauses 4
relevance, norm of 154
representation, semantic 167
restricted quantification 67
Ross, John 167
rules: of deductive system 98f; of deduction 159; of formation 44f; of functional application 136; phrase-structure 46; recursive 46; semantic interpretation 146; spelling-out 136; translation 146
Russell, Bertrand 126, 152, 166

S4, S5 systems 114
salva veritate 117
satisfaction 85
scope 114, 122; of negation 44; of quantifier 64, 68
second-order predicate logic 148f
second-person pronoun 153
semantic interpretation rules 146
semantic representation 167
semantic types 136
semanticists, generative 167
semantics: model-theoretical 73, 159; predictate logic 72f, 83, (formal version) 84; propositional logic 47f

sentence adverbs 109
sentences 132, **148f**; analytic 25; atomic 25; compound 25; counter-factual 39, 120; declarative 170; generic 169; imperative 170; inter-rogative 170; logical analysis of 15f; molecular 25; open 59; single 25; synthetic 25
sentential connectives 26, 124, 169
sentential functions 63
sentential logic 25f
sentential variables 26
sequence 12
set 3; empty 4; power 6; truth- 22; unit 4
set of sets 6
set operations 6, 7
set theory 3
similarity, degrees of 120
simple sentences 24
Sinn 126
situation 22
sortal (or categorial) presuppositions 150
speech, direct/indirect 21
speech acts 170
spelling-out rules 134
Stalnaker, Robert 120
Standard, Theory, Chomsky's 167
statement 21
Stoics 125
Strawson, P. F. 152
strict implication 110–11
structure: constituent 42; overt/covert 166; surface/deep 167
structure-indicating device 42–3
subordinating conjunctions 169
subordination 25
subset 6
sufficient/necessary condition 40
symmetry 89–90, 113
synonymy 23
syntax of predicate logic 58f, **71**
syntax of propositional logic 45–6
synthetic sentence **24**, 53

T system 114

tautology 50f
temporal operators 121
tense logic 121–2
term, individual 60
that-clauses 21, 148
theorem 103
transformation 11
transformational grammar and Montague grammar 146
transitive relation 89–90
transitivity 89, 113
translation rules 146
transparent context 118
tree diagrams 42
triples 10
true analytically, or in all possible worlds 24; or in all interpretations 77f
truth, analytic 23
truth, logical 23
truth-conditions **47**, 129, 155, 162
truth-function 27f, 37–8, **53**
truth-preserving 18
truth-set 22, 111
truth table 30, 50
truth-value 13, **27**, 129, 149f
truth-value gap 155
truth and felicity 153
types, semantic 136, 144–5

union 5
unit set 4
universal instantiation 102
universal set 5
universe of discourse 5, **62**, 170

vacuous quantification 63
value (of function) 12, 133
value-judgements 171
variable: bound/free 64; individual 59; predicate 59; propositional or senten-tial 26
verbs 169
vocabulary, logical 44

well-formed formulas (wff) 44
world: belief 114; ideal 110; possible 22, 108, 160